D1394836

*Perfect Your
Baits*

• PERFECT YOUR •
BAITS

EDITED BY *John Bailey*

The Crowood Press

799.12

First published in 1993 by
The Crowood Press Ltd
Ramsbury, Marlborough
Wiltshire SN8 2HR

A catalogue record for this book is available from the British Library.

ISBN 1 85223 725 2

Acknowledgements
The author would like to thank the following for their ideas, words, advice
and generosity in helping to produce this book: Tony Miles, Keith
Colwell, Chris Turnbull, Gord Burton, John Wright, Jim Whitehead,
Trevor Tomkin, Simon Roff, Frank Guttfield, Neil Pope, Martin Hooper,
Dave Roper, Julian Cundiff, Chris Ball, Lee Jackson, Steve Harper, Ron
Lees, F.J. Taylor, John Watson, Martyn Page, Chris Leibbrandt, Charlie
Bettell, Robin Revell, Jim Hickey, the late David Carl Forbes, the late
Richard S. Walker, and Mike Mee.
    I would also like to thank Paul Groombridge for his excellent diagrams.

Edited and designed by
D & N Publishing
DTP & Editorial Services
The Old Surgery
Crowle Road
Lambourn
Berkshire RG16 7NR

2⊦ 817578

Phototypeset by Fido Imagesetting,
Witney, Oxon
Printed and bound in Great Britain by
BPCC Hazells Ltd
Member of BPCC Ltd

Contents

John Watson, that maestro of pike anglers.

1 *Understanding Bait*

If a fish does not want the bait that the angler is offering, all the tackle and all the rigs imaginable will not persuade that fish to bite. All the angler's patience and ingenuity and expense will be for nothing if what he has on the hook is in the least suspect or unacceptable. This is a simple fact and must surely make bait the most central part of any angler's preparation.

Angling has changed. Back in the days before and after the Second World War, bait was less important. There were fewer anglers and fish were not constantly harassed, caught and generally educated to avoid baits. Also, many, if not most, fish were killed so that their learning process was cut painfully short. Dick Walker's early books, therefore, placed all their stress upon tackle, methods and water craft. In the angling world of those

Maurice Ingham shows that the old baits do work on those Redmire fish.

days, bread, potatoes, maggots and worms were quite enough in the bait box, and the attention of the expert was rightly focused on the technicalities of the sport.

The days when carp would trundle off with a throat full of flake were, of course, halcyon and are not to be repeated. Walker and his friends did not fish cheek by jowl with similarly well-equipped, well-educated anglers. In Walker's world, fish were not caught again and again becoming ever wiser in the process. Fish now are almost afraid of their own shadows, let alone a bait that has spelt danger or discomfort in the past.

It is totally wrong to think that the only area where bait research is important and has made advances is in the carp world. Bream, barbel, roach, rudd, pike and even eels and perch all learn rapidly to distinguish true food from false.

Tench were once considered to be rather dim fish: an angler today clinging to such a concept would see little of old red eye in his net. Tony Miles describes for us here in detail the development of tench baits. While I read it, I realized that a similar progression has gone on in every branch of our sport. Walker's world has gone for good and the future belongs to the man who understands his fish and his bait and the complex, ever-changing relationship between them.

'Over the last fifteen years or so, I've been involved in the tench fishing of quite a few

The crowning glory of Walker's achievement – his one-time record carp.

top-class waters, where the fish have, initially, been under limited angling pressure. However, as news of catches has leaked out, it has been fascinating how modifications in approach and bait have had to be progressively changed in order to stay one step ahead of the fish and keep catching consistently. I'll

concentrate mainly on the bait aspect, both free feed and groundbaits, as well as hookbaits. Hopefully, by putting the findings of my friends and myself into a logical sequence, it may assist less experienced anglers to make some sense of what can be a very confusing subject.

A prime example of how baiting techniques have evolved is with TC pit in Oxfordshire. TC, when Trefor West and I first started fishing it in 1977, was very lightly fished indeed, but when I last fished it in 1986, it had become one of the most heavily fished gravel pits in the country.

The first point to make about a very lightly pressured water is that the tench are obviously not reliant on anglers' baits to more than the most minimal extent and therefore will feed more or less naturally. In gravel pits particularly, the feeding pattern will take the form of groups of fish taking advantage of localized food sources, such as bloodworm beds, and moving on to the next when the first has become temporarily exhausted. In pits, tench shoals are notoriously nomadic for

An old estate lake, very rich in natural food.

precisely this reason. The same behaviour does occur in very lightly fished natural lakes, estate lakes and reservoirs as well, but is usually not as marked, as many of the food sources are far more extensive and will hold more fish longer. The very nature of these waters when compared with gravel pits is that silt beds are more extensive, weed beds are often much more lush and dense and very commonly, deep mud bottoms provide rich feeding almost constantly.

What this means to the angler starting to fish a new tench water where competition from other anglers is limited is that the best way to catch a few tench initially is to create your own localized food supply. If the tench have become accustomed to rooting around in a silt bed for the odd titbit, encouraging them to root about in your groundbait to pick up the odd free offering, including the hook-bait, is simply a logical progression. It was thinking along these lines that led Trefor and I to make the initial approach to TC in a very traditional way: that of presenting large hook-baits, such as lobs or lumps of flake, over beds of cereal feed (groundbait).

Our tench catches in the first two seasons were tremendous. The fish were naïve and once our feed had been found, the fish would gallop off with the hook-baits with gay abandon. No special rigs were required; the fish gave good positive bites to straightforward running leger tackle, or, in my case, to traditional lift float techniques in the margins.

There were a handful of other anglers tenching at TC at that time, but almost all utilized long-range feeder tactics with maggot hook-baits. They certainly caught tench, but not in the same quantities. That was to begin to change in 1980.

Due partly to the big tench we had been catching and partly to the string of big bream that Tony Charlett had reported, opening week 1980 saw the banks of TC packed.

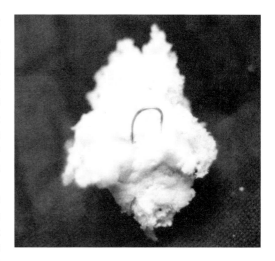

A piece of bread flake.

Trefor and I realized that never again would we be able to fish the water in the peace and quiet we had become accustomed to. There were a great many anglers present to witness our preparations involving the use of a hundredweight of groundbait and hundreds of logs, and the subsequent mammoth catch of specimen tench we enjoyed during an unforgettable first week.

The consequence of that catch was predictable and in no time at all the standard method of TC tenching was the heavy-feed, big-bait approach. A subtle change was, however, taking place which has become much more obvious in hindsight than it was at the time. With a great many more anglers depositing large amounts of feed in the water, the tench population were obtaining an ever-increasing percentage of their feed requirements from anglers' bait. With much more available, they could afford to be more choosy and much more circumspect in the way they picked up food items. As with carp, the more tench that were caught on our big baits, the more wary they became.

The two obvious early signs of an angling approach beginning to lose its effectiveness are the numbers of bites decreasing and fish becoming more finicky. Towards the autumn of 1980 this was very noticeable and although the twitchy bite problem was cured initially by amending the terminal rig to a bolt type arrangement, the lack of bites led to major reassessment of the overall approach.

One of the things, I remember, that occurred to me at the time was that the heavy cereal feed which had proved such a success in the early days, possibly in part because of its novelty value, might, in actual fact, now be proving a deterrent to the tench rather than an attractant. Parallel to the developments in carp fishing, our next move was, therefore, towards smaller hook-baits, principally sweetcorn, casters and maple peas, fished over beds of the same items. Looking back in my records it's quite surprising how limited a life this "pure" particle fishing had, particularly with regard to sweetcorn. Although I had taken several nice tench on corn in 1979, it had been fished as a big individual bait, with

Sweetcorn – the most killing particle bait.

three grains on a size six and with no more than one tin of corn in the groundbait. When I used it in true particle style, fishing a single grain over a bed consisting of two catering cans, only two good catches resulted. Thereafter I caught nothing and this was a mystery to me until one day when I saw several tench move over a bed of corn in the margins. Upon seeing it, they scattered in all directions in panic, quite obviously badly spooked. I formed the opinion then which I've never had cause to change, that although tench were happy to pick up odd grains of corn, they became very nervous of large accumulations of the stuff.

... Hindsight now tells me that the next move should have been to alter the corn somehow by dyeing it or changing the flavour, a dodge that has worked so dramatically for other tench anglers since. At TC I never followed this route, a decision I now regret, as it would have provided an interesting comparison, because most other anglers had taken the particle bait approach to its obvious conclusion: heavy feeding with the swimfeeder and maggots.

Such was the intensity of fishing at TC in the early 1980s that the uninhibited feeding by the tench to the feeder approach was of surprisingly short duration before that also began to lose its effectiveness. During July and August 1982, it was common to have tench blanks and I remember thinking at the time that one of the causes could possibly be that all the anglers were fishing in exactly the same way and competing with one another. Every hook-bait was the same as every other: I had to try something different.

A chat with my friend and first-class roach angler Leon Tandy gave me the answer to the next stage in my tench bait evolution: the simple expedient of flavouring hook maggots.

I'll never forget the first day I used flavourings on maggots at TC. I had fished for two days without success on the feeder, as had the other anglers on the water, including Andy Barker and John Cadd. On the final morning of my stay, I remembered the conversation with Leon and rooted round in my bag for a pineapple flavour I had bought some weeks previously. After flavouring a handful of maggots for hook-bait on one rod, I decided to stick with plain alternative maggots on the other. That way I hoped to form some comparison, assuming that I had bites.

I was not prepared for what happened next. Although I had believed Leon about the efficiency of flavouring, I had not been entirely convinced. That was soon to change. Within minutes of my first cast two pineapple maggots were taken with a bang by a 6lb tench and that was the first of a string of big fish that followed in a hectic two hours. During this frenzied activity, the plain bait on the other rod remained untouched, just as it had over the previous forty-eight hours.

That first dramatic introduction to bait flavouring led to some terrific tenching for a while and fish were caught regularly, not just

on pineapple, but on other flavours, too. In that period, vanilla, strawberry and maple cream also worked well. Obviously, other anglers were working along similar lines to me and within a matter of weeks everyone was on flavourings. Once again, tench catches declined as the fish wised-up to the new approach.

The desire to offer the tench something different led me to revert to a big bait principle at the start of the 1983 season. The tench had not seen much cereal feed over the previous two seasons, so I reverted to that approach, but with one significant difference. I wanted something that could not be ignored by the fish and, therefore, decided upon hook-baits of lobworms or flavoured pastes, fished over cereal feed impregnated with the same flavour and brightly coloured. Talking to the excellent tench angler Alan Smith of Northampton, he told me that yellow feed had proved deadly, so I followed his advice.

The first flavoured paste I tried gave me a memorable catch of tench when other

Few things are more satisfying than a big tench.

A lovely fish comes to the net.

methods failed. Over the previous three weeks, I had caught a fair few fish using lobs fished over feed laced with almond flavour. I had made up a sweet almond paste and, although I had flicked in quite a few free offerings during that time, had not actually used the paste on a hook. On the day in question, I remember I had elected to try flavoured maggots on one rod over the feed and stick to the lob on the other. After about thirty biteless hours, the usually reliable lob-worm was replaced with a large lump of my paste and the results of that bait change were quite spectacular. In the next day and a half I took the largest catch of tench I ever saw at TC, landing about thirty fish. Several bites were missed and quite a few fish were lost in the thick weed that abounded at the time. In all, I must have had about fifty bites and it remains quite the most astounding tench action I've ever had.

The principle of fishing a large bait such as lobs, flake or flavoured pastes over heavily flavoured and coloured feed was one that was

certainly different at the time and was the approach I adopted when first fishing Deans Farm in June 1984. The reasoning was slightly different in that I had been told that the head of fish at Deans was small and I felt that my over-the-top free feed flavouring could be the attractant needed to pull a few fish into the swim. I didn't believe a fancy hook-bait would be required for fish that were lightly fished for and was happy to use lobs. The trick was getting fish into the swim in the first place and that's when I decided to extend the principle to the most pungent flavour I could find. Maple cream was my choice, sweetened to offset any bitterness caused by the heavy dosage I elected to use.

My tenching at Deans Farm, which was sadly short-lived, was one occasion in my angling career when I believe a theory worked almost perfectly in practice the very first time it was tried. On each session, the first twenty-four hours were blank, consistent with the tench gradually homing in on the feed. Thereafter, the swim was full of fish, evidenced by continual rolling, which was quite a rarity at Deans in those days. The first two bites I ever had there to this new approach were two successive personal bests of 8lb 4oz and 8lb 14oz.

Returning to the tench bait evolution that was going on at TC, obviously I wasn't alone in experimenting with flavoured pastes. Other very good anglers such as Alan Smith, Cliff Dean, Alan Wilson and Phil Smith were also working along similar lines and so we rapidly approached the situation where the fish again began to wise up and catches once more began to tail off.

At that time, one angler above all was enjoying more success than any other and that was Alan Smith. I have no hesitation in admitting that it was Alan who let me in to the secret that was to give my tenching another shot in the arm. One day, after he had taken

Bread in pocket, this angler tries for carp and tench.

several fish while the rest of us blanked, he confided in me that he was using "fizzing" baits, by which he meant exactly the same flavoured pastes as before but ones that slowly disintegrated on the hook to form a kind of flavoured halo. This was achieved by the simple expedient of using carefully controlled quantities of finely ground rusk in the paste. Alan's fizzers had given him the all-important edge in offering something different.

He swore me to secrecy at the time, although it was not too long before we were sussed, but many fine fish fell to my own fizzing creations. Almond, which tench certainly seem to like, was again one of the most successful flavours used, followed closely by sweetened caramel. At about the same time, I was also gradually introducing particles to the feed again, but retaining the flavouring and experimenting with cocktail baits. The cocktails that worked best were those incorporating flavoured flake or paste in conjunction with casters, with the feed laced with the same

flavouring and pints of casters also. I remember a terrific night in 1984 when sixteen tench succumbed to caramel-flavoured flake/caster cocktail in the dark hours.

With my experiences since 1977 to draw on and a pattern of bait evolution starting to emerge, it was fairly predictable what the next step was likely to be, as the tench again became used to finding beds of free feed, albeit flavoured. They would again, possibly, become a deterrent. By 1986 this certainly seemed the case and when my association with TC ended, although flavoured paste hook-baits were still catching tench, they were not being fished over carpets of flavoured cereal, but were being presented amongst numbers of other free offerings identical to the hook-baits.

It didn't take a genius to work out what the next short step would be in the progression of TC tench baits, and within a season boilies had replaced the balls of soft paste.

This evolution of tench baits has progressed more or less in the manner outlined here in many waters up and down the country but, of course, no evolution is ever static. The problem will always be there of making the bait different as the fish begin to wise up. Obviously, modern carp baits will extend the life of the boilie approach to tenching because of the diversity of baits available, but the signs are already there that bait presentation is becoming more critical. Making the hook-bait different has always been the key. Once normal boilie fishing tails off, using popped-up hook-bait revitalizes the catch rate. Larger hook-baits are fished in conjunction with smaller free offerings, or normal-sized boilies are offered among beds of mini- or midi-sized baits. Remaining one step ahead of the fish is the name of the game.

What is the next move in this saga? The signs are already there that some of the more heavily fished tench waters are moving towards the modern approach to carping on popular waters, where single large baits are fished in isolation, or perhaps with a stringer of a few others, the thinking being that large beds of free offerings are again causing the fish to spook.

The tench bait topic is certainly a fascinating subject and I wonder what the next move will be, certainly at intensively fished boilie waters like Johnsons or Sywell. I wouldn't be at all surprised if in the not too distant future, the whole thing turns full circle and orthodox methods again become the vogue. Only last summer, a local gravel pit, which is very heavily carp fished but has also produced quite a few big tench to boilies, turned up a real surprise. A local pleasure angler, float-fishing large lumps of flake in the margins, caught a succession of good tench in a few hours one morning when all the hi-tech specialists around him blanked. Food for thought indeed and just one of these fascinating incidents that ensure that tench fishing will never become totally predictable. If it did, I think I'd stop going.'

The most unusual bait I have ever used. This is pig's blood gushing from a bacon factory and when it congealed, the roach and dace loved it!

It is hard to imagine how the importance of bait could be more powerfully stated, and Tony's experiences reveal just how vital an open and inventive mind is in angling. It is very easy to follow the trend and stick with the proven bait but he who dares wins and dramatic success is rarely achieved by following the path of others.

This book details my experiences with bait and those of friends over many years. It is a guide to preparation and usage but it will never be complete and will within twenty-five years or so, seem hopelessly outdated, as articles on bait from the 1960s do now. And when we think of our grandfathers and great-grandfathers using greaves' brains and bullock's pith, it is hard to suppress a smile. Who knows what the future will bring – certainly no one would have predicted boilies twenty-five years ago. Perhaps flavouring and colouring of baits have developed to their ultimate stages but possibly the shape or texture of baits will change. Perhaps we will swing back to the Walker era and concentrate more on how to present baits again. That is the beauty of fishing and of baits: the future is wide open and there will always be things to explore.

2 Firm Favourites

There are some baits that anglers have used for scores of years, if not centuries. They are acknowledged as absolutely safe; that is, that fish will eat them under anything like favourable circumstances. Still, despite their familiarity, there is still a great deal to be said about their preparation and use.

MAGGOTS

I suppose in a bait book it is vital to begin at the beginning and deal with the breeding of maggots. I don't know what percentage of anglers breed their own maggots but I suppose that the number could well rise now that the prices of all baits are rocketing. I suppose further that the specialist angler who really wishes to blitz a water with maggots might well look at breeding his own rather than spending a small fortune at the tackle dealer's. I have no experience myself so I draw on that of Keith Colwell to explain the way that he breeds all types of maggot.

Gozzers

'Some years ago a mate rang to tell me about a great day he'd enjoyed whipping big strong chub out of the River Ribble. "What were you using?" I asked.

"Gozzers," he said. "Gozzers flavoured with Parmesan cheese."

He was a matchman experimenting. Whether he used them again with that particular flavour I can't remember, but it just goes to show what you can try once you're into breeding your hook-baits.

You can breed all the types of maggot you can buy, but the two types worth bothering about are the gozzer and the sour-bran special. These baits are not exclusive to matchmen. Any angler who regularly fishes canals holding bream and roach ought to consider using them. Time and time again I've seen their effectiveness proved to me, and I wouldn't fish the hard canals of the North West for bream in summer without them.

Breeding your own maggots, unless you're a particularly sensitive person, is not a messy procedure. It's not all stink and gunge, or likely to offend your neighbours. The

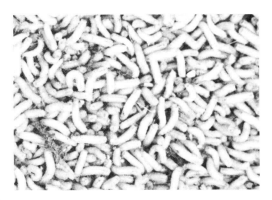

Maggots – the universal bait.

A beautiful crucian carp that fell for a particle bait.

key-word is control – your control. You must control the process, and monitor the development of the maggots, from start to finish. If you do what I've known anglers to do – that is leave a couple of pigs' hearts in a tray down the garden – you will end up with a mess. You'll discover one day a mass of different types and sizes of maggot swarming over the remains of the feed. These maggots are useless, so if you want to breed your own, do it properly.

Some anglers are convinced that the gozzer is the lava of a special fly. It's been my experience that the bluebottle fly lays the eggs which grow into scrumptious gozzers. There is another fly as big as the bluebottle, but with a black shiny colour. I suspect most

commercial maggots are bred from this one, although the best come from the bluebottle. Breeding them yourself, you can make sure only bluebottles lay eggs on your meat.

How do you accomplish this? It's not as difficult as you might imagine. Once you've put some meat down in a sunny corner of the garden, you simply sit down with a cane in your hand and wait. If any shiny-blacks, greenbottles, houseflies or anything more exotic buzz into the container where the meat lies you chase them with the cane. There's no other way. Leave it to chance and you'll end up with the writhing mess I described a moment ago.

I use a deep plastic tub. The meat is put into this on its own. Don't surround it in bran or sawdust until after you know there are eggs from the bluebottle laid on it. Cover the tub with a square of hardboard, but leave a narrow gap for the fly to enter. When you see a bluebottle going in, push the hardboard over so it completely covers the tub and traps the fly inside. It won't take you long. And you will know that you have just one bluebottle inside to lay eggs on the meat. Check there are no gaps between the rim of the tub and the hardboard through which the fly can escape, then place a brick on the hardboard to prevent it somehow being knocked off. If you can now transfer the tub to a shed or garage, so much the better. At least now put it in shade. Leave it for a day. Then check the meat for "blows", which are thumbnail-sized clusters of white eggs. They'll be there, and you'll be on your way to some boss bait.

Before describing the rest of the procedure, some words about the different meats which you can use. The pig's heart is the traditional feed used to produce gozzers, but you can also use liver or chicken. A friend of mine used sheeps' heads once, but I must admit I've never fancied shaking the gozzers out of a freshly picked skull. I have, however, used eels, not the thin bootlaces you catch but ones with some meat on, and the gozzers that come off them are white and soft. Whatever meat you use, the important thing is to make sure you don't get too many blows on it, or blows from flies other than bluebottles. It's worth mentioning that different meats or fish can create different rates of sinking among the resultant maggots. I'll leave you to experiment and see which you prefer.

The fly lays its eggs out of sight. So look closely for the blows. Look in the tubes which go through the heart, or under the wings of a chicken, or inside the mouth of an eel. Two clusters of eggs are the most you need. If there are more than this there probably won't be enough feed to enable the maggots to

In a millpool like this maggots will pick up virtually any species.

grow to full size and you'll be left with runts.

Once you're this far, knowing there are just two clusters of eggs from a bluebottle laid inside the pig's heart, there are two ways to proceed.

One is to leave the meat in the tub, and put some dry bran or sawdust inside. Remember you must keep the hardboard cover in place to prevent more flies blowing on the meat. This is why I said use a deep tub: to make sure the growing maggots don't overheat, or run short of air.

The other way is to transfer the meat from the tub to newspaper. Loosely, though securely, wrapped in a couple of pages of *The Times* and left for five or six days in a corner of the shed, your gozzers emerge from the meat and clean themselves up in the creases and crumples of share prices and scandals about insider-dealing. It must give them that killer-instinct, because once on a hook they ruthlessly hoodwink the wariest of fish.

If you leave the meat in the tub, the maggots will crawl from it into the bran, which will clean them. Gozzers take about six days, depending, naturally, on the temperature, to mature from eggs to full size. It's no use leaving them longer in the hope that they will grow even bigger and more succulent because they stop feeding after some time. Some anglers prefer to take them off the meat earlier, believing that a small gozzer is more effective on the hard-fished canals. So, once you have some already crawling in the bran, or the folds of newspaper, you can shake the remainder out of the meat. Sieve away this old bran and put the gozzers into some fresh and slightly dampened bran. Now you have one of the best canal baits; one which many anglers believe is indispensable when it comes to catching bream and roach.

If you can get a bluebottle to lay its eggs on chicken, the maggots you'll get will be very white and soft. I've found that the greenbottle – which produces the maggots we call pinkies – homes in on this meat much more quickly than bluebottles, but don't be put off trying if chicken's what you have available. Gozzers bred on liver have a faint yellow colour; not quite as buttery as annato, but nevertheless almost as attractive to roach.

Whatever you nurture them on, gozzers have a way of making usually shy fish take them boldly. I don't know how an organism as unsophisticated as a fish develops the discernment of a gourmet but that's exactly what it seems like. You can fish for hours using commercial maggots – even with those you've diligently scoured – maybe getting the occasional finicky bite, and then swap to a gozzer to find yourself suddenly getting a bite off every cast of quality bream which don't want to let go.

Some anglers, like my mate mentioned in the beginning, try adding extras to the feed while the maggots are eating and growing. You can add all sorts of exotic food flavouring or colours, but don't use too much or add it too early in case it actually puts the maggots off feeding. I prefer my gozzers unadulterated. If I want coloured maggots, I buy them coloured, or dye shop-bought whites myself, after cleaning them with Turmeric. This removes their greasiness and makes sure the dye stains them properly.

Sour-bran Specials

This sounds like an American football team. They certainly beat the hell out of the fish in canals! They look like feeder maggots, only they're two or three times bigger and whiter and softer. It will take you longer to start a nursery of sour-brans. But if you get the first lot going in a shed, you've only got to put down another bowl of souring bran to attract more blows.

Use bowls or trays. Soak two or three pounds of dry rough bran (which is sold in most pet shops). Spread this evenly in the bowl or tray, and leave it in the shed or shade until a crust forms on the surface. Some anglers soak the bran in milk, but I've had just as good results using water for the initial soaking. You'll probably have longer to wait for blows off the fly responsible than you did for those from the bluebottle, but at least you don't have to hang about to chase away any unwanted flies. As far as I know, only this particular fly chooses to lay its eggs in sour bran. And I've never known a bowl to be overblown, either. Sometimes, once you have the maggots feeding on the bran, you can tell by their size that they are two different batches. But all you need do is take off the mature maggots and transfer the others, in the bran, to another bowl you've been preparing.

Big roach have long been associated with maggots or flake.

Check for blows by lifting up the edge of the crust which forms. These eggs are tiny, so tiny at first you might think you're looking at a smear of whitish dust, but you'll soon get the knack of distinguishing them. All you need do now is wait for them to grow. When they're fully grown, just scoop out some bran with them still in it, transfer it to a bait box and rush off to the canal. Brilliant boss baits are sour-bran specials.

That's the way I breed them. To make sure I have them for the early days of the season I lay out two bowls of bran during the first week of June. I've known anglers who have complained that they just can't get the blows but, after talking to them, learnt that they've been trying to get them on a blob of sour bran offered in a small bait box. This was the trouble. Once they offered two or three dry pounds soaked in water and milk, the right flies came along and procreated. So if ever you seem to be waiting too long for a hatch of eggs, try offering more sour bran. A bait box full isn't enough, apparently.

Other anglers I know have bred excellent sour-brans off a wild mix of rotting vegetable matter. They add cabbage leaves, potato peelings, all sorts. One guy even trained his cat to pee on the bran. Ah, the lengths to which some people go to win matches.

However you procure yours, believe me you have the boss canal bait – for coloured,

Maggots have been the downfall of many a barbel.

summer canals at least, where bream and roach predominate. You usually fish them over a patch of feeders in groundbait, so they must look like a fat version of the feeders that bream can soon become preoccupied with. Whatever the reason, they work, and if all your canal fishing has so far been confined to using commercial maggots, you will be gratefully surprised at the difference this boss bait will make to your catches.

The only problem with sour-brans is that they turn more quickly than other maggots into chrysalides. So, even in a fridge, you can't keep them much longer than four days.

Pinkies and Feeders

Finally, a word about pinkies and feeders. There's no point breeding these yourself. The pinkie is the lava of the greenfly, which sometimes might lay its eggs on chicken intended

for gozzers if you're not careful. It's a good canal bait, but attracts mainly small fish – roach and gudgeon. Unless you can't buy them, and discover there are 1lb roach in your local cut which will eat nothing but pinkies, I wouldn't consider them a hook-bait. Likewise with feeders. I've caught 3lb bream on a bunch of feeders offered on a size 22 hook, but I probably wouldn't have resorted to them if I hadn't been competing in a match. Simply because a 3lb bream, even on a hard-fished canal, is more likely to succumb to double gozzer or bread flake. Feeders are, however, essential for feeding with ground-bait when you're after bream. And that goes for lakes and rivers, as well as canals.

There you are, then. Breeding your own gozzers and sour-bran specials isn't difficult, messy or too time-consuming. Don't be discouraged from trying by anglers who like to shroud fishing in an air of mystique. Traditionally, the gozzer fly is a special fly which emerges only during dark to lay its eggs in a fresh pig's heart. It sounds good, only, if it were true, surely the species would have died off long ago, there being a general lack of fresh pig's hearts lying around the country at night.

No, the bluebottle produces what we call gozzers. And it will lay its eggs in warm sunlight, like most other flies, and on any meat whether fresh or slightly high. It's for your own convenience that you choose to use a pig's heart, a piece of liver, breast of chicken, or even a sheep's head – not the fly's.

Sour-brans, however, prefer sour bran. You can farm them off various rotting vegetable matter, but it's just as simple and, I believe, more convenient, to use plain rough bran mixed with water and milk.

Both baits will catch you good fish from hard, coloured waters in summer. Both are indispensable for matches on canals whether you're fishing a National or competing for your club's trophy. Now you know how to breed you own, you'll never have to leave home without these two boss baits.'

Every coarse fisherman has used maggots in his career and the variations on the theme are consequently enormous. Maggots are used dyed in bait cocktails along with corn or flake, in singles, doubles or vast bunches on hair rigs for carp or tench or on size 26 hooks for bleak. An example of 'maggot ingenuity' is Tom Pickering's development of the floating maggot. Basically, a handful of clean maggots is dropped into a bait box containing one eighth of an inch of water and left for anything up to half an hour. By this time most of the maggots will be swollen and will float. Three maggots prepared in this way will support a forged size

16 hook, perfect for tench, bream, roach, rudd or small carp. Tom has suggested the use of Racing Tortue 'Nacrita' as a foot length because of its excellent floating qualities. Three-pound breaking strain line is probably best for this type of fishing.

Maggots prepared in this way absorb flavouring readily if one or two drops are added to the water that they soak up. Meat and liver flavourings appear to be excellent but as Chris Turnbull found out in the summer of 1992 the flavour is fairly immaterial. He personally has just had great success on chocolate and strawberry flavourings. In fact, it seems that the use of the floating maggot has revolutionized Chris's fishing. A rig fished without the floating maggot has gone untouched for days whereas bream and tench have fallen regularly to the buoyant bait.

Bream adore maggots, often with a sweet flavouring.

His own rig includes four floating maggots on a size 12 which are just enough to make the hook float. He uses a Drennan Specialist hook – the Super Specialist is just that little bit too heavy. He fishes them on a 2in hook link so that they sit proud of the bottom. The maggots are sucked in, they turn and hook themselves on the weight on the 2oz lead beneath. Easy!

Chris has watched tench and bream feeding in close quarters in clear water and he is convinced that twitch bites are not all they seem to be. He sees tench in particular sucking and blowing over a bed of maggots. They suck everything in from the bottom – maggots and rubbish. Anything that doesn't taste or feel right is immediately blown out again. This is why twitch bites occur: the tench feels the hook, or at least the hooked maggots do not enter the mouth properly and the fish immediately ejects. The angler on the bank is either unaware of what has happened or notices only a slight twitch.

Chris believes that the buoyant maggots go into the mouth of the sucking tench in a much more natural fashion and are therefore accepted. Of course, if casters are the chosen hook-bait, it makes sense to sort out floating casters to use on the hook in the same way as preparing buoyant maggots. Three floating casters will support a size 12 or a 14 hook with ease.

The only slight problem that has been discovered is that in extreme heat the maggots seem reluctant to float (Fig. 2.1). Perhaps taking a small flask of iced water might be the answer in these conditions. It really is worth going to this type of trouble for what can be a revolutionary bait.

The bonus of maggots from a matchman's point of view is that they attract all sizes of fish. That is their disadvantage to the specialist angler, especially fishing a river. Says Andy Orme:

A poly-ball to make maggots buoyant

Fig. 2.1 A buoyant maggot rig.

'Maggots are good but also expensive and are the worst bait for attracting the unwanted attentions of nuisance fish. Many an angler has invested in several pints and then been plagued by bleak and minnows. Maggots are also quite light and in strong currents can get washed out of your swim easily.

This lightness can be a problem and a flow and maggots are best fed with a dropper or a feeder to get them direct to the river bed' (Fig. 2.2).

CASTERS

One of the most important match baits and particle baits for many years has been the chrysalis of the turned maggot, best known as a caster (Fig. 2.3). For all fish species the

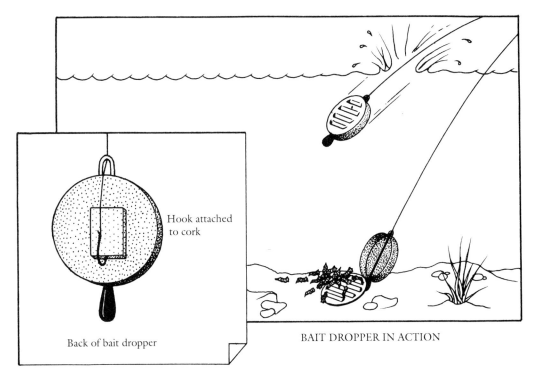

Hook attached
to cork

Back of bait dropper

BAIT DROPPER IN ACTION

Fig. 2.2 The bait dropper.

caster has proved a killer, especially when fished over a bed of hemp. The casters are expensive unless you produce your own. Keith Colwell explains how:

'Casters vie with maggots as the universal bait. So good are they at catching fish, some anglers have attributed them with almost magical powers. There doesn't seem to be any species which has not fallen to the caster's spell, though their use is associated mainly with the capture of roach.

The anglers who discovered that chrysalides actually sank for a time during their development were on to a winner. Match-fishing reputations were built on the effectiveness of the caster by wily anglers who kept their sinkability to themselves as long as they could – which wasn't long in the fierce

competition of the matches. That sinkability was the most important discovery, of course. Many anglers used them on the hook before that discovery. On balmy summer days when we were kids poaching on ponds on Lord Derby's estate, we'd take all weights off the line and hook on a chrysalis and catch rudd and perch on them from between the lilies. But that was before we knew anything about the need to feed. That was before we learnt that there is a time when floating chrysalides actually sink.

Nowadays you can order casters from tackle dealers by the gallon. Everyone uses them, whether for snicking six-ounce roach out of the canal, or hauling stones of barbel from the river. I've heard some top-class anglers say it's too much to do our own casters, and that what you produce is no better

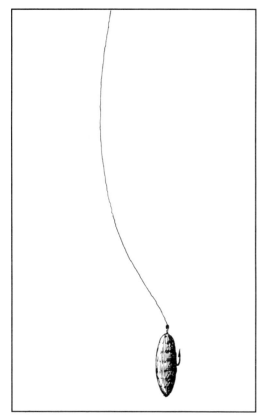

Fig. 2.3 Single caster on the hook.

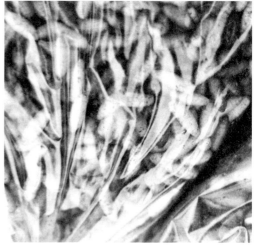

Shop-bought casters in a polythene bag.

than what they can buy anyhow. I disagree with them. You don't need four pints of casters for most fishing, and what you can produce for yourself will be, after a few practice runs, probably superior to what you buy. It stands to reason, after all. Dealers are in the mass production business. They will do their best to sell you fresh, quality casters,.but they can't really compete with the angler who turns a few pints for his own use. The way things are, some tackle dealers would be grateful if they didn't have to spend so much time looking after casters, so you won't be doing them a bad turn, or denying them much profit (most dealers sell bait as loss-leaders, anyhow) by producing your own.

The quality of the casters you produce depends on the quality of the maggots. You need large whites, preferably. Coloured maggots can produce good-quality casters, but for the very best results use large whites.

In the summer, maggots you buy will start to change into chrysalides within three to five days. For the best casters, you need to control this transformation, and you accomplish this by using a fridge. I'm presuming you buy your maggots a week before you need the casters; if you want them sooner, all you need do is clean off the old sawdust and put them in a shallow tray among dampened bran or clean damp sawdust, and allow them to change in the shed or garage.

You have more control, however, when you allow the maggots to change either in the fridge, or after being stored for two days in a fridge. Maggots which change in a cool temperature make large, dumpy casters. So after a couple of days in the fridge set around the 40°F (4°C) mark, check the maggots' progress. Some may have changed to white casters. If so, take them from the fridge and put them through a sieve. What casters you

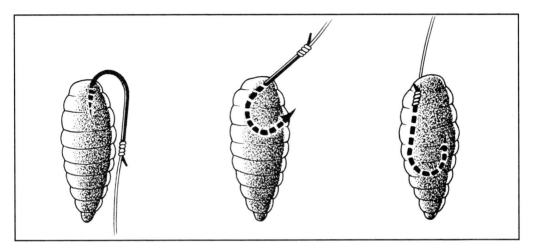

Fig. 2.4 Hooking a caster.

Carp adore particles like casters, maggots or corn.

have will be white or just taking on a faint tinge of orange. Wash these in a colander and place in a plastic bag and return to the fridge.

The plastic bags you use for storing casters ought to be opaque. If you put casters in a clear plastic bag some of them will develop yellowy-brown scorch marks. I don't know why this happens, and, although fish might not be bothered by the unusual colours, the casters certainly look less attractive to the eyes, and this affects your confidence in them as a boss bait. So use opaque plastic bags to keep your casters in.

During the next couple of days the maggots will be slowly changing in the bottom of the fridge. Check their progress as regularly as you can. Put them in a sieve when you see there are casters to be formed. Wash and bag the harvest. If you're finding red casters among the maggots in the fridge at this stage, great. It means you have the whole process in your control, which is precisely what you want.

Sometimes, though, you may have had a few dozen light-coloured casters off at this stage. All you do is remove the tray of maggots from the fridge and let them get on with their metamorphosis at room temperature. After being restrained in the fridge, this process accelerates once the maggots hit some warmth. This is the advantage of using a fridge, because after some practice, you'll develop the knack of knowing just when to put them in the fridge or take them out so that you end up on the day before fishing with two or three pints of maggots all turning a lovely red colour virtually together. Keep passing the maggots through the sieve, and washing and banging the casters as they come off. The morning of your fishing trip should see you with the last rush of casters and very few maggots left. And any remaining maggots will change during your trip to the venue.

Those casters you've been bagging will have continued to deepen their colour in the fridge. The last thing you can do before you set out is to tip the casters into a bowl of water to sort

A nice wild carp that fell for a small bait.

out any floaters. There shouldn't be too many. You can discard them, or carry them separately for use on the hook (Figs 2.4, 2.5 and 2.6).

This method is, I reckon, the best. But it can be time-consuming. If you regularly fish with casters it becomes easier because you can have three or four pints of maggots in shallow trays more or less permanently in the fridge, under your control.

An alternative way to produce them is simply to leave two or three pints of large maggots in a shallow bowl of water. Casters stay alive by breathing, so submerged in the water their development is completely arrested. In fact, if you leave them for too many days in water they will drown and when the day comes to go fishing many of them will be a dirty greeny-brown colour. You may still catch fish on them, but the sight of them doesn't actually inspire you with confidence. The way to escape this problem is to remove those you've kept for a day in water and put them in a plastic bag in the fridge as above. If you choose to keep them in water until the day you require them, then at least drain them and carry them to the venue dry. Most of them will probably still be alive, and during the trip their colour will deepen from white and light orange to a uniform redness.

Remember, keeping casters in water for more than a couple of days will kill them. The innards turn sour. I have known anglers catch fish on casters as poor as this, but for the best results you must be able to use a fridge. Most serious anglers I know bought themselves second-hand ones and set them up in the shed or garage. Considering how indispensable fridges are for storing most baits, the cost is negligible.

Never try to rush maggots into changing. An angler I knew was desperate for casters for the following day, and so placed a bowl of maggots in front of the fire. All he did was ruin the maggots, and the few casters he got were horribly shrivelled and wrinkled. The only time

Fig. 2.5 The hooked caster for confident fish.

you may wish to speed up the process is during winter. Then the tray of maggots can be placed in a warm room. Airing-cupboards are ideal as long as no one objects.

The main aim is to be in control of the process. This will come with practice at watching the development from the soft, white-coloured chrysalis through the light orange-coloured stage, to the last crisp redness. In

Hook casters parallel to avoid line twist

Fig. 2.6 A pair of hooked casters.

summer you need to keep a close watch on the maggots because they can begin to turn at any time and proceed at a gallop. That's why a fridge is vital if you want top-quality casters.

So there you are. Buy large white maggots, preferably on the day they are delivered to your tackle shop. Replace the old, slimy sawdust with fresh stuff or rough bran and dampen it. Place them in shallow bowls or trays. If you keep two or three pints of maggots in a deep container, those at the bottom will be warmer, and the transformation into casters will be uneven. Control when they begin to change by keeping them in the fridge. After that, control the rate at which they change so that you get an explosion of casters coming off two days before you need them at the top of the fridge, while any maggots you may have in there will be on the bottom, in the salad compartment. Practise this until you get to know when to put the maggots in the fridge and when to bring them out into the warmth and you'll end up with casters as good as the top match anglers use.'

Of course, most people tend to buy casters direct from the tackle dealer, already turned and sold in plastic packs. They are an expensive investment and it is important to look after them. Once you get the bait home take them out of the polythene bag and put them in a bait box. Ideally, the casters should fill the box right to the top but if there is any space left, fill it with sheets of damp newspaper. Then it is important to make everything airtight with a sheet of clingfilm between the box and the lid.

At the water, light-coloured casters that have only just turned can be safely left in the open air for four or five hours. However, keep an eye on them and when they begin to turn dark, cover them with a skim of water. This will stop them turning any further and keep them fresh. These wet casters are also quite useful as they tend to cling together and can be catapulted quite far as loose feed, very useful on windy days or when extreme accuracy is essential.

Indeed, casters make the ideal feed bait. Don't forget that they are totally immobile and, unlike maggots, cannot crawl away into the bottom silt or weed. Casters stay where you put them unless the flow moves them or fish eat them. Casters are also excellent in balls of groundbait because, having no movement, they cannot break up the ball in mid-air. In fact, groundbait can be absolutely impregnated with casters and still reach its mark. Some of the old fenland bream anglers were in the habit of crushing the casters into almost liquid form and mixing this with the groundbait to give it a very distinctive smell and texture.

Their theory was that it was irresistible to the big fenland bream. Remember not to put too many casters into the groundbait at once. Those that are not thrown in immediately very quickly become floaters and rise to the surface. Put fresh casters into each ball of groundbait as you make it up.

Casters can be an absolutely killing bait for most species (Fig. 2.7) and they do have the habit of attracting the biggest fish of the shoal in front of you. Chub can at times go absolutely crazy for the bait and will eat half a pint per fish if given the chance. I have caught chub, opened their mouths and just seen their throats awash with the husks of gobbled bait. Casters are also a brilliant barbel bait especially fished in conjunction with hemp. There is no doubt that the big bottom feeders love the

A heavily fished water often responds well to caster in winter.

taste of fresh casters and soon take them every bit as eagerly as corn. Mass particle baiting with casters works equally well for carp, the only problem being that many gallons are needed to get a swim really alive to the bait – a very costly business unless you are prepared to riddle off turning casters at the bank side.

Tench and bream are both caster-mad and, surprisingly for supposed bottom feeding fish, will often come up towards the surface to pursue them. Again, it is often the case that the biggest fish will leave the bottom first and begin to look for the casters dropping through the water. For both bream and tench, there need to be a fair few fish in the swim for this to happen. Competition is essential but once either species have the taste they will take them almost as soon as they hit the surface.

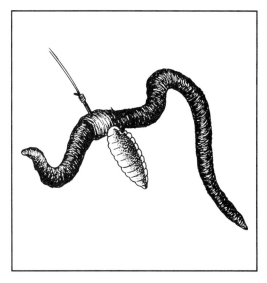

Fig. 2.7 A killing cocktail.

Chub will gorge themselves on caster.

BREAD

Bread is one of the oldest baits, it is very cheap and easily obtainable. These facts alone do not make it the highly successful bait that it is. It used to be reasoned that bread was so attractive to fish because of wheat in the fields that line rivers and lakes. This is hard to understand, not least when roach in an industrial canal adore bread! The simple fact is that bread is highly visible and that alone is one of the most vital considerations. A roach, for example, will quite easily miss foodstuffs on the river bed only six inches from its snout. In fact, when watching roach feed, it can be hard to understand how the species exists at all. A large, white piece of flake appears to be seen reliably often from up to two feet away under reasonably clear conditions. At night, the visibility of bread is even more central to its success rate.

Equally certainly, bread also releases a significant and attractive odour. Using roach as an example a second time, the shoal will move quite deliberately across a river to a carpet of bread groundbait that definitely cannot physically be seen. From up to ten or more yards downriver, the roach seem to be aware of the presence of a significant amount of bread and begin to look for it very actively.

Once fish find bread they will generally eat it avidly, providing of course it does not carry unpleasant memories for them from the past. Chub, roach and rudd will at times gorge themselves on the stuff. Barbel can become real bread eaters in the October to March period, especially when the water carries some colour. There is no doubt that carp can be caught on bread today, as they always could be. Indeed, now that bread is so little used by carpers, the chances are that it has not been so potentially effective for decades. On several occasions for me, a rod fishing bread has comprehensively outfished the rod with the most

A huge roach of almost 3¾lb that fell to bread.

up-to-date boilies. Each time this has happened in the November to February period during cold snaps of weather.

A major attraction of bread is that it can be fished in many different ways, according to conditions and to the species of fish sought.

Bread Flake

Every angler who has caught good roach in his time swears by bread flake. For well over twenty years, however, discussion has centred on whether bread is best taken from a sliced loaf or the old-fashioned tin variety. Traditionalists stick with the unsliced crusty loaf and certainly it looks better and more wholesome. In my own opinion, there is nothing to beat the modern 'plastic' sliced loaves that predominate now on the supermarket shelves. A medium sliced loaf is absolutely perfect and remains fresh in its polythene wrapper for days. Freshness, more than anything else, is the key to successful flake fishing. It is simply impossible to put flake on the hook successfully if the bread is in any way stale. Certainly, to leave the loaf out in the sun on the river bank for even an hour spells absolute disaster.

Simply pull the crumb gently from the loaf and lay the hook in a fold around the size of an old 10p piece. Carefully but firmly press the bread over the shank and the eye of the hook. It should not be moulded in any way for if the bread is fresh enough it will cling to the hook through the casting and for at least twenty minutes in the water. Once the flake is in the water it tends to expand, an important consideration when deciding upon the size of the bait. However, thoroughly wet flake is a very soft, soupy bait and a roach or even a dace can suck in a surprisingly large amount at one go. Bites tend to be very definite indeed and the strike should be firm and steady. Generally I fish flake on hook sizes 8 or 10, only going to a 12 or 14 for dace and down to a 4 or a 6 for carp.

Flake can catch virtually any species in any conditions: it can be trotted for chub, legered for carp, float fished for tench, quiver-tipped for barbel or fished on the drop for dace. It is light enough to rest on top of weed and will not sink into the finest of muds or silt. It was once considered to be a bait of the summer-time but this is nonsense. In fact, flake probably works best on both rivers and still waters in mild, cloudy winter conditions. It is truly a bait for all seasons and for all species.

Bread accounted for this, my first 3lb roach.

Bread Paste

Bread paste is another old bait and one around which controversy circulates. There is little doubt that it is best made with stale bread but many anglers prefer to make it up at home before the fishing session, using water from the tap. This I do not do. My own, quite unproven, belief is that the chemicals in tap water can be detected by the fish and make the bait objectionable to them. It is far better, I believe, therefore, to make up the bait at the waterside and use the actual element in which the fish swim. Take the crusts off the loaf and put the white bread in a bowl. Add just enough water from lake or river to make the bread go soggy. Drain all the surplus water from the bowl and tip the contents on to a clean cloth or tea towel. Hold the ends and squeeze as much of the moisture as possible from the mixture. Open the towel and pound the mixture until it is no longer sticky. Now it should be smooth, white and pliable. It should hold well to the hook but should not mask the point on the strike. If the paste is too wet, add a little more dry bread to the mixture. If it is too dry, simply add a little water until the right mixture is achieved.

For centuries, anglers have liked to add things to their paste in the belief that it makes it more attractive to the fish. Honey is an old favourite as is peanut butter. Many of the modern carp bait flavourings can be used as can the various dyes – yellow and red especially. Crushed hemp can often be mixed in with the paste, or sweetcorn juice or even tinned cat food. A sprinkling of grated cheese also gives the paste added consistency and flavour. Custard powder gives a nice yellow tinge to the paste and also enhances the smell. Bovril is an old favourite additive though some have always preferred Marmite. The variations are simply endless and the major question must be whether they are necessary

at all. Possibly, at times, they do give paste an edge if the water is very clouded, for example, and extra scent is needed. It could just be that particularly educated fish will respond to something a little different. Above all, there is the question of confidence: the angler who believes in his bait will fish just that little better than the man who simply puts bread on the hook when nothing else seems to work.

Bread Crust

The very fact that the late Owen Wentworth fished bread crust so exclusively for his beloved Stour roach must be recommendation enough for this bait. Many years ago crust was known as 'Cube' and the time-honoured method was to cut the bottom crust off an unsliced loaf leaving a layer of crumb intact. This long length of crust was then dampened and left under two weighted boards overnight. Once fishing, the strips were merely cut into the desired hook size. Great care was taken to keep the crust away from the sunlight because once it dried out it was totally useless.

There is no doubt that this method of fishing crust would work as well as ever but the more usual way today is merely to pull a piece of crust from a fresh loaf and push the hook

Bread is the bait that men have used for centuries.

through the crust so that the point comes up into the white crumb.

Crust is, of course, very buoyant and shotting patterns must overcome this. It is as well to check the bait out on the margins before settling down to fish.

Crust is a very successful bait shotted for roach and chub but it is also useful in still waters, especially where soft mud or dense fine weed is a problem. It was to overcome the problems of disappearing baits that Richard Walker pioneered the balanced crust over forty years ago. In his classic book *Still Water Angling*, Walker writes:

'Where the bottom is very soft indeed or covered with silkweed, it is possible to fish a crust sunk, with a running lead which should be as small as possible, on the cast, stopped by a shot an inch or more from the hook, according to the depth of the silkweed or mud. The buoyancy of the crust keeps it just above the level of the mud or weed. If the right proportions of crust and paste are chosen, it can be made to sink very slowly and will rest on the surface of the mud, or on silkweed without sinking into it. The bait, if properly balanced, takes a minute or two before beginning to sink. The crust should be put on the bend of the hook and the paste moulded round the shank. The bait then comes to rest with the line emerging from underneath, where it is not encountered by the lips of a fish investigating it.'

It was Walker, too, who developed the method of floating bread crust for carp. Of course, this technique had been known before but it was Walker and his group who took it to refined lengths. Walker concentrated particularly on margin fishing his crusts. He discovered that carp were very keen to visit the windward shore of a lake at night to browse on washed-up titbits. He would position himself there at dusk waiting for the patrolling big fish, his crust dangling from the rod tip, ready to be lowered once a fish appeared.

Believe it or not, this method still works very well! On a great many waters carp become very used to floating pieces of bread and, now that carp anglers seem exclusively switched on to 'high tech' baits, a piece of floating crust is often something that carp feel very safe with. Floating crust also picks up its fair share of big tench and rudd and, though the bait does seem old fashioned, it is unwise to neglect it entirely.

Bread Punch

Punch is simply a piece of bread taken from a sliced loaf and compressed with a commercially available tool into a small pellet upon the hook. For many years bread punch was one of the favourite methods of roach fishing on the northern canals. It was primarily a method of catching numerous smaller fish but it also accounted for its fair share of large ones. Through the 1960s, during the maggot revolution, bread punch fell out of fashion. In the 1970s it began to re-emerge but only recently has it become a winning method again. This renewed interest is reflected in the tackle shop where there are now several excellent punch kits for sale.

Further punch literature is not available but *Coarse Fisherman* magazine recently ran an excellent series on punch fishing by the well-known match angler John Wright. For hooks John uses Gamakatsu 6315s in sizes 18 down to 22. These are his normal hooks but if he were to use really large bread punch, usually when after chub, he would switch to a Drennan forged match hook which is just that little bit more robust.

For bait, John says, 'You need two loaves of Mother's Pride, one thin sliced, the other medium. If the match was being fished on a prolific venue where the roach are of a good stamp, then I would get one medium sliced and one thick. Take a few slices out of each bag for hook bait.'

The rest of the loaves – the vast majority – are used to make up the liquidized feed. John continues:

'The rest of the two loaves go into the liquidizer, after you have removed all the crusts. Once it has been in the whizzer, run it through a maggot riddle and then through a squatt/pinky riddle. Put the residue back into the liquidizer and repeat the process. Now freeze it – I do mine the day before a match. Last thing at night, take it out of the freezer and defrost it! Yes, I know you've only just frozen the stuff but you see, by freezing liquidized bread, it seems to separate it and make it slightly powdery, unlike freshly liquidized bread which is very cloggy. By doing all this the day before a match, the end product still retains its original fresh, bready smell that roach love. If you leave it in the freezer for any length of time it tends to lose its aroma and pulling power. It's only a small point but lots of little points can add up to a big score and, in the world of match fishing, that's what makes the difference between a winner and the also rans.'

John is certainly a perfectionist and to each match he also takes his own home-made very fine brown crumb to use as feed with the punch method. He describes in detail the way that he makes his own crumb:

'I am often asked about the method I use to make my own groundbait so I thought some may benefit from me explaining this. Believe me, it's well worth all the time and trouble spent doing it, as you will never be able to buy the like over the shop counter. Stage one. Firstly, any stale, or left-over bread you acquire should be dried out naturally. I dry

Bread punch is often a winning match method.

mine on a shelf in the kitchen, next to the airing cupboard. I leave mine until it is completely dried out and is like crisp bread. The bread that I use varies from sliced bread to french bread, rolls, brown bread, uncut loaves, in fact anything so long as it's bread. When it is dried out, I bung it in a carrier bag. When I've filled up two or three bags stage two begins. This is the equipment you'll need; one oven, one tray, one pair of tongs, one liquidizer, one large bowl, one flour sieve and a couple of bags.

Right, put the oven on to full blast, then fill it with loaves of bread, placed on the shelves. When the bread has turned golden brown, take it out of the oven, using the tongs (because it gets hot) and place it on the tray to cool down. Throw away any bread that gets burnt or black around the edges. Burnt bread tastes bitter and is no good for our crumb. When it has cooled down a bit, break it up into small pieces and half fill the liquidizer. Give it a really good spin and then run it through the flour sieve into the bowl. Anything left in the sieve simply goes back into the liquidizer – no waste. Repeat the process until you have finished the whole consignment. You will now have a bowl full of fresh, pure, extra fine brown crumb. Give the contents a good stir round and bag it up.'

These feeds John introduces into the swim by means of a pole cup, the amount depending on the swim and the conditions. There is far more to the punch method than I have included but at least these are the baits involved. It is interesting to note that what John says has relevance far beyond match fishing alone. Recently I found some very large clear river roach that were very wary of any bait put to them in the normal manner. It was only when I introduced liquidized bread to them that they began to show any eagerness to feed. A large piece of punch drifted through the cloud after one hour of sparing feeding then did the trick in the shape of a 2lb 1oz fish. All this goes to show just how versatile and successful a bait bread is, and the angler who uses his loaf thoroughly is bound to succeed in the end.

Floating Crust for Chub

There are three things to say right away about crust fishing on rivers for chub. Firstly, this is the most exciting type of angling I've ever known: the bow-wave, the hit, the flurry of spray and the tightening line are unforgettable, pure adrenaline-pumping stuff. Secondly, crusts can sort out the biggest chub on a river. This is not always the case but it does happen very often, especially on rivers where the method is not much used.

Thirdly, you must understand that there are some rivers where chub will not come up for crust at all. There is no obvious reason for this and the rivers that refuse to co-operate are thankfully few. I have fished crust from the Wensum in the east to the Wye in the west and I'd say that ninety per cent of clear rivers do respond. But do remember that remaining ten per cent that can be a disappointment. One such river used to be the Waveney – it looked perfect but it was useless.

Ideally you will need two or even three large crusty farmhouse loaves. It saves time at the waterside by preparing the loaves at home. This is simple: skin the loaf of its crust with a sharp knife to produce several score of chunky crust pieces. Do not cut them all to a uniform size. The smaller ones should be half an inch square and the larger ones can be as large as two inches square. I said square but it's a good idea to leave many of them ragged or misshapen. There are days when the chub will want plenty of variety. And, don't throw away the flake inside. You might find that it is useful to take it along in its own separate plastic bag.

The perfect rod will be light and long with a steady power: light because you have to hold it for a long while; long because you will need to mend the line as the crust trundles

A piece of crust to tempt any chub.

downstream; powerful because the rod will need to cope with three- or even five-pound chub in weedy quick water. I use the Drennan 13-foot tench float rod but any beefed-up match rod will do nearly as well. Oh, a point here: it pays to grease the rings of the rod to allow the line the easiest possible passage.

Any fixed spool reel will do but again it is a good idea to grease the rim of the spool. Take two spools, one holding 4lb line and another 6lb line. Make sure there is plenty of line on the spool because sometimes the crust is trotted at least eighty yards downriver. A selection of hooks between sizes 4 and 8 and a landing-net pretty well complete the outfit ... I nearly forgot a single spool of Drennan double-strength line, either 4 or 5lb breaking strain. This is the beauty of crust fishing; you travel light and you keep on the move and you catch good fish.

It is essential to find a quiet stretch of river. Even one or two anglers will spoil the method so sometimes a long walk out into the countryside is necessary. Failing that, get up before dawn and make sure you are on the river at first light.

Ideal water should be clear, quite weedy, perhaps on the shallow side with a reasonable flow. It's always nice if it is tree lined but this isn't vital. Surprisingly, a really straight barren stretch of river can often hold a lot of chub. The fact that there are none of the usual snaggy, chub-holding places seems to bother us more than it does the fish.

Begin by taking a dozen crusts out of your bag and throwing them into mid-river. It is simply, then, a task of following this flotilla of brown and white downriver until they attract a group of chub or simply disappear into the reeds and marginal snags. Keep a good

The great F.J. Taylor nets a good chub.

distance from the bank as you follow them so that any chub will not be spooked. When chub see the crusts, you are left in no doubt. They simply surge after them and often the takes can be heard fifty yards away. A dozen crusts can disappear as if by magic in thirty seconds or less. Once you have found them, feed in more crusts and get them going crazy before starting to fish a crust on the hook.

At first, especially when the chub are not used to the method, your crust will be taken however clumsily it is presented (Fig. 2.8). You will find the fish simply go wild for it and this is the time when big catches are made. Enjoy this while you can, for the chub very quickly wise up to what is going on and soon your hooked crust is the one piece that is not taken.

When this happens, the first thing is to check that your line has not gone on ahead of the bait. This creates drag and makes the crust behave unnaturally. Now it becomes essential to mend the line with great care making sure that it does not pull the crust off its course downriver. This is where the long rod comes in and you might even have to grease your whole length of line to make sure it does not sink and make mending impossible. If the fish continue to be wary, use a six-foot hook length of the Drennan double strength. The drop in line diameter will often bring a few more fish to the net. When both these ploys stop working, it is really time to think.

Try very large crusts or very small crusts. Try threading a crust on to the line and push-ing it twelve inches from the hook where it is held in place by two leger stops. On the hook put a piece of flake so that the crust actually acts as a float. While the chub remain wary of your crust, the flake will almost certainly be taken a few times before this trick is

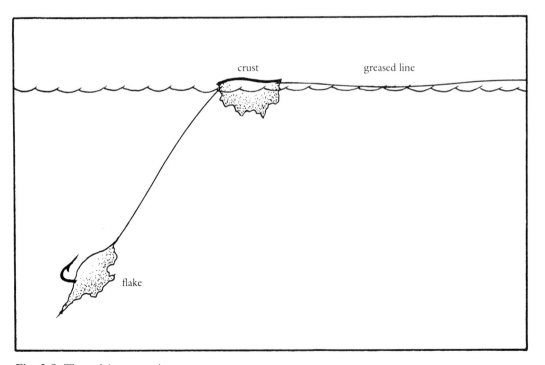

Fig. 2.8 The uplying crust rig.

discovered by the ever-wary chub mind. Sometimes it can help not throwing in free offerings: if there is only the hooked bait going past them, there is nothing else with which to compare its behaviour.

When you have thought and thought and gone through all the variations, there is one further method to try. Choose a night of a bright moon and get down to the river in the silvery darkness. Fish in exactly the same way as you would in the daytime and very soon you will locate feeding chub by both sight and sound. Believe me, chub will go mad for crust in the dark. You do not have to watch your hooked crust intently – it will be taken with such force that you will feel it at the rod, even when the fish is fifty or sixty yards away!

You will find that if you ring all these changes you should keep ahead of the wiliest chub shoals all summer long. It really is a thrilling, effective method that keeps you on your toes and makes you think from the moment you try it. A couple of last points: a long-handled landing-net is often useful to reach out over wide reed fringes. This is a very mobile method of chub fishing, so do not try to keep fish as you catch them – it is far better to let them go immediately and you will find they won't spoil the fishing but sulk somewhere in the margins. And do remember to take the empty plastic bags home once the crust and flake has gone: cattle could otherwise be the victims of your carelessness.

CHEESE

A lot of the older, traditional baits are no longer used simply because they were poor ones and have long been overtaken by modern alternatives. This is not the case with cheese, a golden oldie that really does work excellently on very many days. Right until the end of the 1960s you would never find any general angler who did not have a piece of cheese somewhere in his basket. What caused the decline in its popularity I do not know but somehow, for whatever reason, cheese slipped out of favour. A mistake! There is no better time to experiment afresh with cheese than in a long hot summer or even well into the autumn when fish are still feeding well. Cheese and warm water have always gone hand in hand and there are many hot days when cheese beats bread, maggots or corn out of sight.

Cheese has always been regarded as a chub bait first and foremost and certainly there are times when they will go mad for it. In 1979 I actually fed a chub one pound of cheese and it ate every scrap, including the last chunk with a size 4 hook in it. The little pig weighed 5lb 2oz ... presumably 4lb 2oz before this cheese spree began!

Remember, though, cheese is equally effective for roach. There are times that bream, tench and carp take it eagerly and, rather unexpectedly, some of my better crucians have fallen for pieces of soft cheese paste fished on a size 16 hook over a bed of hempseed.

During the 1950s and 1960s the most commonly used type of cheese was a plain ordinary Kraft cheese slice. From mid-June, I guess many a little village shop unexpectedly sold out of their entire stock in days! Kraft was easily available, kept for ages at the bottom of a basket, was easy to use on a hook and was devastatingly effective for river roach and big stillwater bream. Chub adored large pieces on a size 6 or 8, and tench would pick up a corn-size blob on a size 14 in preference to bread every time. They still do! It's time for a secret! Kraft is still a superb bait. In summer 1991 I used Kraft seriously for the first time in twenty-five years and found it dramatically effective on the River Bure and several local still waters. Working out at around 6p a slice

Baits for everybody.

there cannot be any cheaper, more effective baits around.

One of the delights about cheese fishing is the almost infinite variety of cheeses available. A recent count at my local supermarket revealed almost seventy cheeses that I guess would make good, perhaps even brilliant baits. The question is, of course, which to choose and when and for what. If you want to use straight cheese then its 'hookability' is important. Some cheeses are simply too crumbly or too soft to endure casting. This is where some of the more rubbery cheeses such as Dutch Edam or Gorgonzola are very useful.

Though this is nothing like a rule, I personally have found roach and tench prefer the slightly milder cheeses, whereas I have had carp and chub go for very full flavours indeed – so full, in fact, that they have made me go green every time I have looked in the bait box! Blue cheese just cannot be too high for

chub and if you can get a piece on to the hook and into the water then it is as near a guaranteed bait as possible. My grandmother fished before World War I and she always told me when I was a child that the best cheese for Trent chub was stuff with maggots in it. I think they bred women tougher in those days.

Cheeses not firm enough to stay on the hook themselves can still make excellent pastes. First, I get a sliced white loaf, cut off the crusts and add cold water until the bread goes soggy. I place the mixture in a clean cloth and drain off the water. The next step is to pound the paste until it is pliable and no longer sticky. Now I can begin to work in the cheese little by little. Cheeses like Cheddar, Stilton and Cheshire are all excellent, either grated or simply crumbled into the mix. Obviously the more cheese introduced the stronger the flavour. Ideally I make it soft enough to come off the hook when it is retrieved at the end of the cast – a simply perfect bait for chub, roach or barbel.

Cheese can just be loose-fed into the swim like any bait but do be careful not to overfeed. It is very heavy and fills roach especially, very quickly. An excellent alternative is to use liquefied cheese in a feeder. Take some rotten cheese paste that has stood in the sun for a couple of days and put it in a food liquidizer with some water. This will produce an evil-smelling, devilishly effective liquid. At the bank, soak strips of foam rubber in the concoction, place them in a large feeder link and cast gently but rapidly into the swim. The liquid gradually oozes out of the foam to create a compelling cloud hanging over the bottom. This method is particularly effective in slow-running or slow water but remember, you will need extra lead to sink the buoyant foam rubber and it pays to practise a couple of times at the water's margin.

Certain conditions, even after October, simply cry out for cheese: if the river is running high and warm after long periods of westerly winds and rain with visibility down to six inches or less, and chub and roach are hunting by scent rather than sight. It is now that little beats a few pieces of ripe cheese fished on the edge of an eddy and close to a snag. A bonus barbel is also far from unlikely. These big fish will be sheltering from the main current and feeding hard on drowned lobworms. In their frenzy, something as pungent as cheese is equally liable to be sucked in.

The warm weather is replaced by anticyclones and the night temperatures plummet. Both the rivers and the still waters become crystal clear and, as the temperatures drop, fish move and feed less and less. It is at times like these that on the point of dusk, small pieces of cheese are sufficiently attractive to produce some response. Great as my faith is in bread flake, I have to admit that when water temperatures dip to the low forties or less, cheese takes over as the bait for big roach.

POTATOES

The potato was in many ways an early boilie. It was round, hard and had the skin to avoid the nibblings of smaller species. Sadly, the potato was not nearly as adaptable as a boilie and once carp were caught on one they soon began to treat others with caution. However, it could just be that today so few carp have seen potatoes that they are worth a try once more. Certainly, in their heyday, potatoes were an extraordinarily good bait and time should not have changed that.

The carp anglers of the 1950s and 1960s used to hunt out small new potatoes or tinned potatoes. There was discussion on how long the potatoes should be boiled and whether they should be peeled. A general preference seemed to be for potatoes that were boiled just hard enough to stay on the hook and yet soft enough to remain very attractive. The skin frequently seemed to give the potato a flavour that the carp liked.

Obviously, there were potato techniques developed in those days. For example, I think it was F. J. Taylor who pioneered the use of the sliced potato. If the potato is cut into slices of about a quarter of an inch thick then these will flutter down through the water and, with any luck at all, land in soft reed instead of disappearing into it. It was, again, I believe, Jim Gibbinson who needed to cast the potato long distances and found that a piece of crust on the bend of the hook would keep the bait intact throughout a long cast.

Going back again to the 1960s, it was Peter Stone who wrote glowingly about the use of chips as bait for chub. I took him seriously then, as I do now, and fished chips a fair bit during the later 1970s with very good results for that species. What I also found was that barbel showed interest – though I never caught one on a chip – as did bream, roach and even

Even today potato could be worth a try on waters where it has long been forgotten.

tench. A chip certainly looks, tastes and smells attractive and it could well be a very useful change bait on certain waters at certain times.

WHEAT

Any walk around an average lake will reveal that about ninety per cent of anglers are using maggots and perhaps just a few have a small can of corn or brandlings somewhere in sight around their pitch. A similar walk thirty years ago would almost surely have shown a high percentage of pleasure anglers using wheat. In those days wheat was considered to have two advantages: it was cheap and it caught larger fish than most other baits. This is still the case today regarding price and, I guess, selectivity.

Any serious attempt to fish wheat will begin at a corn store. It pays to buy in bulk as the price obviously comes down accordingly. Look for big, fresh kernels. Try to avoid those that look dusty, wrinkled, cracked or smell fusty.

For a normal pleasure session three to four cupfuls of dry wheat will prove quite sufficient. First wash the wheat and then let it soak in cold water overnight. Next morning, bring the grains to the boil and simmer them until their white insides show through the parting skin. Then switch off the heat at once for if the grains are overcooked they glue together into a useless stodge. Empty the pan back into the sieve, pour cold water over them and then bag them ready for freezing.

For normal fishing purposes, wheat is fished very much like maggots or casters but do remember that wheat sinks quickly and also fills fish fast as well. One grain on a size 14 hook or two grains on a size 10 or 12 are generally about right for roach, tench, or bream.

Wheat also adapts well to the specialist approach. Prebaiting in large quantities can prove dramatically successful for carp, bream and tench. All three species develop a real fixation for the bait given any chance at all and it could well be the bait to crack that particularly hard water. For carp, of course, two, three or four grains can be fished on a hair, though this is rarely necessary for bream or tench. (In any case, for tench, a long hair provides more problems than answers.) Bream become absolutely addicted to wheat once they have begun to eat it. In fact, if enough wheat is put into an area over a long enough time, the bream shoals will hang around for weeks hoping for more of the stuff.

I have not tried this, but I suspect that wheat would work dramatically well for barbel as well as for other species. Certainly it would sit very well over that almost obligatory carpet of hemp.

PERFECT YOUR BAITS

BANANA

During the 1960s banana was the 'in' bait for carp and took over to some degree from potato and flake. Certainly, it did seem to have many advantages. It was easily available, easily prebaited and seemed quite acceptable to the species. However, in the present age of boilies and particles banana is once more redundant although I would not be at all surprised if it continued to work moderately well on waters where carp have forgotten all about its drawbacks. The other fish that takes banana quite readily is the chub, naturally, and it can be fished successfully in much the same way as any other large bait.

While on the subject of fruit, another old favourite is the cherry. This was once a noted chub bait and indeed I caught plenty of chub myself from the Wensum on black cherries in particular during the 1980s. However, with the price of cherries rocketing, there are much better cheaper baits now available. As for the other fruit baits such as apple, pear, olives, blackberries, pineapple and strawberries, well, I feel in all seriousness they can be discounted. The only time I would now contemplate their use is if for some reason, a glut of the fruit is going in the water,

Slices of banana could bring some surprises today.

perhaps for example outside a canning factory or at harvest time. In my experience, fruit is an acquired taste and is certainly too expensive to prebait extensively.

MEAT BAITS

Luncheon Meat

For many years now it has been known that luncheon meat is an excellent, often deadly, bait for most fish species, especially chub, barbel and carp. It is a bait that works well used as a single lump cast to a fish in a snaggy area. It gives off enough smell and oil to trigger that fish into accepting it without any other inducement.

Most commonly it is loose-fed into the swim, diced into similarly sized cubes. Mostly, these cubes are around half an inch to an inch square and the amount used obviously depends on the amount of fish present and their type. A cube of luncheon meat is often a deadly bait fished over a bed of particles, generally hemp, but maggots and casters work almost equally well.

It is also possible to use luncheon meat in conjunction with a kind of 'rubby-dubby' of bread mashed up with luncheon meat, sweetcorn and its juice, maggots, hemp and casters. In fact, anything that will contribute to the oily, smelly slick spreading over the swim can be added. Chub and carp in particular will respond in an almost frenzied manner to this approach.

Generally, luncheon meat is cut into cubes at home and then stored either in a bait box or a plastic bag in preparation for the fishing session. Hooks obviously depend upon the size of the bait being used: and a one inch square cube will sit nicely on a size 4 hook whereas a half-inch square cube is generally used with a size 8. Smaller cubes – say quarter

The different brands of luncheon meat all have their own qualities.

of an inch square – can be used on a size 12 for tench, roach or bream.

In fact, watch any angler using legered luncheon meat and it will be invariably cut off in the cube form. Ron Lees, my old friend and expert on the Severn, questions this: 'A better way of using this deadly bait is to tear it off in loose pieces. In this way, tiny particles will break off under water so giving off a constant form of loose feed.' Ron is correct. Chunks of luncheon meat are attractive because they do disintegrate and give off their own attractive particles. Cubes, however, are very deadly at first because a fish homes in on their size and shape. The cube has a visual attraction all of its own. However, once the fish become wary of cubes, then a change of shape – into the rough chunk – often prolongs the life of luncheon meat.

A problem facing the luncheon meat angler is which of the many brands to buy. Some are definitely inferior and are best avoided. Nothing is more disappointing than to arrive at the river or lake only to find the luncheon meat is so soft that it will not stay on the hook and is useless. Other meats have little flavour or smell and rarely seem to attract anything. Over a long period I have tested a number of brands and now feel quite confident to draw some conclusions which should prove helpful.

Nisa Chopped Ham and Pork This is a reasonably priced bait which claims to have a 90 per cent meat content. Certainly the luncheon meat is of a good firm texture. This allows it to withstand reasonable casting and thirty yards is achieved without any real fear of losing the bait. It also has a very good smell and colour. It sinks well and can be used in relatively small pieces as loose feed in even quite a rapid current. My only reservation with Nisa is that the bits of meat and fat in the mix could mask the hook point and blunt any strike. This has not happened to me but I feel it remains a possibility.

Derwent Chopped Ham and Pork This is very cheap with no claim made about meat percentages. It is soft in texture and breaks up very quickly, especially in heat. However, it does have a strong, highly spiced smell which did make me persevere with it further. It has another interesting property: it is buoyant! This makes it useless as loose feed, apart from as a floater perhaps, but it is a good bait to use to counterbalance the weight of the hook. In fact, a small piece will keep a size 8 hook swinging off the bottom, almost like a pop-up boilie. For these reasons, Derwent is worth buying occasionally and, again, Ron Lees

Small cubes of luncheon meat pepper the surface.

offers some advice which will help to keep this soft meat on the hook when casting: 'My tip is to thread one small piece up the line, place another on the bend of the hook, pulling the former down until it rests on the latter. This will assist with the problem of soft meat coming off on the cast.' This useful advice really works well with Derwent and allows it to be cast twenty yards with ease and confidence.

Spam This is on the expensive side of the luncheon meat spectrum but it claims to contain prime cuts of quality pork with a minimum percentage of 90 per cent meat. It possesses a very firm, even texture with little to impede the hook point on the strike. It sinks well, an attribute which makes it excellent for loose feed. It also has a pleasing, light colour which sets it apart from most of the other makes. It is probably, therefore, one of the best average luncheon meats available to the angler.

Princes Pork Luncheon Meat This tends to be moderately priced, partly, presumably because it contains only 80 per cent pork. It is very pink and smooth and has a peculiar rubbery texture all of its own. Princes has one very useful characteristic: it is a slow sinker which makes it excellent for use in still waters over a soft weed bed. In fact, it will come to rest on the top of flannel weed without sinking from sight at all. Princes is also my favourite meat for float fishing. Loose-fed pieces drift downstream enticingly and a piece trotted three feet under the float is taken without any suspicion at all.

Plumrose Pork Luncheon Meat Plumrose is frequently seen on the bank, partly because of its moderate price and its very good smell. However, it is rather soft in texture and does tend to break up in the heat so its casting distance is limited. It is, though, quite a fast

sinker which makes it useful for rivers and deeper swims close into the bank when far casting is not important.

Celebrity Pork Luncheon Meat This is a Danish brand containing 80 per cent meat and is very reasonably priced. It is one of my favourites for it is very pink and smooth but with a surprisingly firm feel to it. It also sinks very well, giving a long casting distance with little fear of it shedding the hook in flight. Indeed, when I can find it, it remains one of my favourites.

Bacon Grill This is an expensive bait for one containing only 80 per cent meat. However, it has the most distinctive smell of all, presumably a factor in making it one of the most popular carp baits of the 1970s and early 1980s. It tastes very heavily smoked and leaves a real tang in the nostrils. It also has a very firm texture and gives a casting distance in excess of virtually all other luncheon meats. It is quite a slow sinker as well so that it balances hooks very nicely into the bargain.

Spar Luncheon Meat This is readily available and very economically priced, containing 80 per cent meat. It possesses one of the pinkest colours of all and is quite firm enough to

A piece of sausage can work wonders.

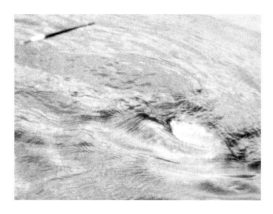

This carp was caught on meat under a float.

cast a good way though it does break up a little bit during the heat. It has a good taste, smell and texture. For some reason I have found Spar particularly effective in the winter, though don't ask me why that should be!

On several occasions I have cubed Spar luncheon meat and fried it for a few minutes in a pan until it has developed a hard, attractively smelling crust. The process seems to make it more buoyant but in the water it gives off an even more attractive flavour and chub seem to love it prepared in this fashion. Again, in the winter, when the going is hard, it is probably worth taking this extra little bit of trouble to give you the edge.

All luncheon meats are best kept in a fridge as long as possible before fishing so that they are as cool and firmly textured as possible. Strangely, the converse can be true for meat thrown in as groundbait. I have found that meat which has been out a couple of days in the sun on the bankside and is very smelly and squashy pulps up very well and sends an irresistible slick down river. It's a messy business but a highly effective one. A friend of mine once left his meat so long that it actually had maggots working in it before he used it as groundbait. He said the results were spectacular but frankly I'll leave him to it.

Bacon

Bacon is a bait of which I have absolutely no experience whatsoever. Only for a short period in Autumn of 1967 did I try the bait a few times on the River Dane for chub. It did work moderately well on the few occasions I used it. The initiative to use bacon was not mine, however. Around that time, in the now defunct magazine *Fishing* I had read an article by a certain Jim Whitehead entitled 'Bacon – a bait that sorts the men from the boys!' The author wrote:

'Few chub of less than ten pounds have taken bacon whilst me and my friends have had plenty over three pounds and few over four pounds. Our "control" rods, fishing worms or cheese paste or flake, have taken a more normal selection of fish. The bacon really does seem to be selective.

If you want to try it, buy yourself a small piece of bacon. The end of flank is cheap and is our usual choice. The aim is to get a piece which has a good layer of fat and of rind, but a couple of streaks of lean lower down. Boil this piece for about twenty minutes but don't overcook it – you don't want it falling off the hook.

Leave the cooked bacon to cool overnight. If you can put it in the refrigerator you will find it very easy to slice in the morning, but this is not an essential in the winter months. Cut the bacon in slices about one eighth of an inch thick and cut your baits from these rashers. The baits can be any size up to one inch or more wide and three inches long and the hook is slipped just under the rind, which runs along the narrow edge. The bait looks most peculiar dangling from a number 6 hook, and I've had some very odd looks directed at me at times, but ledger the bacon in your usual way and wait for a firm bite.

We have found it unwise to try to hit the first knock. Almost invariably there comes a good second pull and in all cases our chub have been hooked in, or near the lip.

The bacon should be slightly buoyant, or at least have only a slight negative buoyancy, so that it can work in the stream. It may be this fluttering action which has aroused the predatory interest of occasional pike and eel. Such catches may become more common as the swim gets regularly fed with bacon by the discard of damaged pieces and dumping of unused baits. We have never groundbaited or deliberately fed bacon into a swim but obviously in our regular spots it has slowly become a familiar food and has worked particularly well where worms and cheese are overfamiliar.'

Bullock's Pith

It must be one of angling life's modern little tragedies that bullock's pith is no longer with us! Let me explain. Way back in the seventeenth century, pith was proclaimed as one of the best available baits for chub. In 1622 Robert Venables wrote: 'The pith or marrow in the bone of an ox back, take it out carefully and be very tender in taking off the tough outward skins but be sure you leave the inward and tender white skins safe and untouched or your labour is lost. This is an excellent bait for chevin (chub) all winter long.'

The enthusiasm of Venables was matched throughout the nineteenth and into the twentieth century. The advice was to cut the tough skin off the marrow and then cut the marrow itself into small lengths with a pair of scissors. Apparently, the pieces nearer the neck were the sweetest and most acceptable and sometimes a little steaming toughened what was a very tender bait. It seemed that the pith was best threaded on the line and then slid down on to the hook for a secure hold.

The bait had rave write-ups. It was supposed to turn chub on in even the dourest freezing conditions. It was a bait 'second to none' and every old angler worth his salt went to the trouble to secure it. I think most anglers of my generation, brought up in the 1950s and 1960s, fell under the spell of the old pith legend. I never actually used the bait myself, or even saw it in use and it was only while researching for this book that I began to investigate the possibilities thoroughly. A tragedy! Pith is denied us! Since the outbreaks of mad cows' disease, it is obligatory for all butchers and slaughterers to dispose at once of the carcass and offal of the animals. Apparently, it is illegal now to sell the pith that so delighted anglers of old and it looks as though any attempts to reintroduce the bait are doomed by legislation.

GROUNDBAIT

There are many different forms of groundbaiting, all designed to entice the fish into the swim and to persuade them to start feeding. One of the simplest and most primitive forms of groundbaiting is simply to drag a swim. This age-old method involves throwing in a rake head upon a rope and dragging it back towards the angler through the bottom mud, silt and weed. The idea is that a cloud will be created in the water and all manner of foodstuffs thrown up from their hiding places. Tench have always been suckers for this approach, but it also works on roach, perch, bream and carp as well. It is simple and cheap and efficient and I do not know why it has fallen out of use to such a great extent. Indeed, I can't remember the last time that I saw somebody drag a swim except to remove excess weed or snags. Perhaps a problem is our overcrowded fisheries where one man creating any sort of commotion would instantly be jumped upon. Still, the method is there and it does work, and if the circumstances

The type of water where dragging a swim is important.

allow it, the drag should never be forgotten. Older books have gone into great detail to describe how to build a drag of your own. I hardly think this is necessary and any old rake head, bought for a pittance at a car-boot sale or market, will do the job fine. The length of rope needs to be around ten or fifteen yards, depending obviously on how far you can throw the rake head, with a little bit left over for safety. Throw the drag out half a dozen times until the water in front of you colours up and then introduce your bait samples. Fish will quickly move in to the area.

Today, one of the simplest and most common forms of groundbaiting is the scattering of bait samples into the swim. These serve both to draw down passing fish and also to get them used to taking the food that is on the hook. Again, this type of groundbaiting is quick and easy and also very effective. The skill lies in gauging the exact amount of bait to put out: too much bait and the fish over-feed and lose interest; too little bait and there is not enough to hold the shoal and they wander away. Striking the right and fine balance is a matter of experience and of having some knowledge of how many fish are in the swim. Half a dozen pieces of loose bread flake are often quite enough for a roach shoal of one or two big old fish whereas a pound of sweetcorn is often not nearly enough to hold a shoal of bream or a dozen large carp. The best advice, probably, is to work the swim up until fish are bubbling and rolling and then keep them interested by introducing particles of bait little and often.

Loose-feed groundbaiting has over the years developed into the concept of prebaiting. The aim here, like ordinary groundbaiting, is twofold: firstly to attract fish to an area and secondly to wean them into accepting hook-bait. It is simply the time scale that is different. Prebaiting by its very name, implies feeding the swim some time before the actual fishing session takes place. To serious anglers, prebaiting is now a necessary risk. The chosen swim is prepared carefully: weeds are cleared, the bottom is perhaps raked clear of rubbish, and overhanging branches are tied back. Feed is then introduced on a regular basis over a period of days or even weeks. Ideally, the bait should be visible on the bottom: if it continues to lie there untouched, a change of swim or bait is called for. Generally, if possible, it is best to introduce bait in the evening as fish are more likely to find it than the venue's waterfowl.

There are many examples of long-term, intensive baiting programmes that have yielded vast rewards. I was first made aware of the possibilities of prebaiting in the late 1970s when Arthur Clarke, a very well-known specialist angler of the time, set about a Norfolk pit with sweetcorn. He prebaited with scores of pounds of corn – amounts have grown legendary with time – for several weeks before the season began. His results were phenomenal. His swim boiled with fish and for seventy-two hours he caught big bream seemingly ceaselessly. What is more, the lake's notoriously difficult carp population succumbed and, though he lost a lot of fish on the stagings in front of him, he still landed more in three days than most anglers had done in three seasons.

Prebaiting can be successful even if not taken to such extreme lengths. A few scatterings of chosen bait before the season begins

Evidence that at least one man believes in prebaiting.

or before a campaign starts, will alert the fish to the possibilities of a bait, especially if it is a little new or different on the water.

Prebaiting can also serve to indicate whether fish are in fact present. This is especially useful on the typical lowland river of today where fish are few and far between. If highly visible pieces of bread flake are put into a swim in the evening and have disappeared by first light, then it is highly probable that they have been taken by fish. The swim is therefore worth investigation and a few sessions. If, on the other hand, the bread is still there in the morning, then fish almost certainly have not passed through during the night and, probably, if this process is repeated on a few occasions, the area is barren and can be discounted.

The most traditional form of groundbaiting is to use brown or white breadcrumbs. They should be mixed with water and thrown or catapulted into the swim. The concept is that the fish see the carpet of food and are attracted to it, finding some titbits but not so many that they ignore the baited hook. Many

Martyn Page baits up a swim heavily.

anglers still use breadcrumbs as their sole type of groundbait. Most often it is mixed firm in a shallow open bowl. The bait should be put in first and the water added until it begins to feel spongy and is easily moulded into balls. With a little practice, it will be found that these balls will hold together in the air without breaking up until they hit the water; then they filter gently and steadily on to the bottom.

Light groundbait explodes much more quickly on impact and is mixed less damp. It should be wet enough to hold together in flight but so soft it breaks down into fine particles when it hits the water. This creates more of a cloud than a carpet, perhaps more attractive for fish swimming in midwater.

Groundbait covers the reels and rod handles.

For very deep swims, or water where there is a fast flow, a heavy groundbait mix should be used. The process is the same as the medium mix, only the balls are squeezed tight to increase their density. The balls keep together well in the air and plummet pretty well intact to the bottom.

In practice, good groundbaiting is rarely as simple as this sounds. Firstly, in very clear water larger, more wary fish may be afraid of crossing an unexpected light or brown patch on the bed. If the light is right, it is quite possible to see tench, for example, actively avoid the whole area.

Secondly, it is very easy to sour a swim through days or weeks by the use of too much breadcrumb. It must be used sparingly or it will be left to fester on the bottom, acting as a positive deterrent. I once put too much breadcrumb into a bream swim and it was still visible ten days later ... with an accompanying absence of fish.

Thirdly, breadcrumb alone is hardly an attractive food for any fish species. All the non-predators will eat it, but not with enthusiasm. Nor does crumb have a strongly effective odour, capable of pulling fish shoals from afar. It is possible to use additives to enhance the taste and smell of groundbait. Most of the carp boilie flavours can be added, especially the sweeter varieties. Alternatively, or additionally, the mix can be dyed red, green, yellow or even black to blend in better with the bed and scare the fish less.

By far the most common and useful additive, however, is a large helping of hook-bait samples. In this way, the groundbait becomes more of a carrier, allowing hook-bait samples to be introduced at long distances. Any hook-baits can be used: casters, hemp, corn and wheat are typical. With maggots and chopped worms the mix needs to be quite firm to resist the wriggling action that could break the balls up in flight.

Ivan Marks – one of the founders of modern groundbaiting.

Intelligent groundbaiting is a vital part of all angling success. The skill lies in gauging precisely what the water and its fish stocks require. Overfeeding and underfeeding are equally harmful. The key is to put out a mix that the fish will find attractive and stimulating and which does not arouse any suspicions. Crumb, perhaps flavoured or even dyed, loaded with succulent food particles, placed accurately, carefully and strategically in the right amounts at the right times, is a vital aid to catching fish, but to get all this right does take thought and practice. All manner of variations are possible; for example, Tom Boulton, the famous Essex matchman, once described his 'curtain effect' groundbait. This was mixed medium to firm the pieces of crust, and floating casters were stirred in so that they broke free on the bottom and rose enticingly to the surface. In this way, there was a constant stream of goodies from top to bottom, enough to stop any passing shoal of fish in its tracks.

Everything so far has been very traditional, but around 1980 leading matchmen concluded that Continental-type groundbaits were far superior to our own. In 1980 itself, Germany won the World Championships and the feeling here was that their overwhelming success was largely due to their groundbait and techniques.

Ivan Marks in particular came home impressed and began a series of experiments with fish in tanks and later with the aid of skin-divers in a small gravel pit. By watching the reaction of fish to different substances, Marks formulated 'Secret Squirrel' which contained seventeen different ingredients. The success of Secret Squirrel was instant and it was not surprising that from then on manufacturers entered into a race to produce groundbaits with high attractant qualities.

The average angler can easily get confused about which groundbait to buy and when to use it. After all, in recent months, tackle-shop shelves have been packed with new makes and different recipes and this trend will continue. Many of the companies that produce groundbait are doing their best to educate anglers with easy-to-follow instructions on the packaging. Some of this may be sales talk but there is generally a genuine desire to help the customer spend his or her money wisely and use the correct groundbait for the job in hand. Some of the modern groundbaits have specifically designed purposes. For example, Euro UK Groundbaits have marketed Deep Red Lake, which is designed for fishing in depths of over six feet; Fast Feeder Plus, which has been formulated to break down in water,

Samples of modern groundbait.

Anything exotic is worth trying.

quickly giving fast dispersal of the feeder's contents; and Canal Match Mate, which was originally designed for gudgeon but has been found to work well for most other species. The famous Marcel Van den Eynde company has also put specific groundbaits on to the market. High-Pro Specimen mix is high in protein and formulated for use on prolific carp fisheries or any waters using large stocks of specimens such as bream, chub and tench. Included in the groundbait are particles of flake large enough to attract and hold bigger fish. Or again, the same company produces Active Feeder which is primarily intended for use in an open-ended feeder on both still and running water. The ingredients used have been blended to produce a very active groundbait which works quickly once in the swim. How about Surface Cloud? This has been designed for use as an aid to attracting and encouraging fish to feed near to the surface. It contains very little food and can be used with or without loose offerings and mixed to catch fish feeding high in the water.

One British angler who has thoroughly investigated the Continental groundbait scene is Trevor Tomlin. With Ian Heaps he travelled to France to the factory run by Sensas. This is a company run by some French brothers, primarily grinding seeds for the cosmetic industry. However, it is the residue of this process that interests anglers. The brothers found that they were constantly pestered by anglers for the remains of the crushed copra coconut shell, maize or rape. In fact, Sensas use more than a hundred ingredients, and scores of them were of interest to French anglers.

The French have always been front runners in groundbait technology, largely because the style of pole fishing demands it. The Continental way is to bombard a swim with ten to fifteen balls of groundbait at the start of the match. All the competitors are fishing bloodworm at a limit of ten to fifteen yards and so the only difference between the competitors tends to be the composition of their groundbait. The man who can find the right groundbait for the fish and the water is likely to be the winner. Taste, colour and activity all play their part and that is why Sensas became so central to the French match angler. The British reliance on brown crumb seems almost in the Dark Ages by comparison.

In France, Trevor told Sensas about UK conditions. Together they compiled lists of ingredients that seemed suited to British waters, each serving a different purpose. Some were merely attractors with little food value, some were quite filling and some had tremendous actions, while others were to give a taste that all fish respond to, for example vanilla or coriander.

The research began to pay off and gradually a whole range of groundbaits was established to suit every situation a match angler, or even a specialist angler might face in the course of their season. The fisherman who wants to build up a bag of bleak now has the ability to put out a cloud with little feed in it that gives the small fish cover and security from any possible predator.

The angler who wants to take roach in midwater now has a groundbait that breaks on the surface and forms a semi-cloud in mid-water. The strong taste of ground or grilled hemp really attracts roach and puts them in feeding mode. The river angler now has a groundbait that is firm enough to take all the ingredients to the bottom where it will break up slowly and release a stream of tasty particles.

There is now a heavy groundbait for deep stillwater swims. The groundbait hits the bed and particles lift up enough to entice the fish. There is constant activity down there and a twitched bait often provokes a savage response. Remember that fish spend a lot of their time looking for insects to emerge from the mud and silt and rise to the surface to hatch out. This groundbait simulates this type of effect.

For bream, there is now a groundbait that presents a mass of coloured particles on the bottom. Bream like to take their time, browse and only choose what takes their fancy. This attractive bed of bait is perfect for their finicky nature. The 'Explosive Feeder' is perfect for chub as it works on the surface or on the bottom and is richly hemp-based. It carries casters very well and, when put in a feeder dry, explodes when it hits the bottom in a compulsive cloud.

Sensas have pioneered a groundbait for carp that is changing the face of match fishing and could well be adapted by the specialist angler. It is only recently that carp have come to the fore in matches and so Sensas had to develop something for them. Two experts were called in and a carp groundbait was manufactured. When it came to this country, Mark Downes had one hundred and twenty-seven pounds of carp using it for the very first time. The concept is that carp are a greedy fish that are active on the bottom, in the middle and on the surface. Therefore the groundbait gives them a rich feed and works at all these levels. When mixed dry it hits the bottom and

Billy Lane – once world champion angler – never underestimated the
importance of groundbaiting.

large particles of maize and pieces of bread
rise enticingly to the surface. If the fish are
being sought for exclusively on the lake bed,
it is best to mix the groundbait and riddle off
the large particles. These should be soaked for
twenty minutes until they are large and will
not rise to the surface. Trevor is of the opinion that in these highly boilie-orientated days,
a new approach could work very well for the
specialist angler.

What about those lakes increasing in number where no groundbait is allowed whatsoever? Aldersons of Bury, Lancashire have
marketed 'Black Cloud' which can be used
both for introduction to a swim by catapult
and in an open-end swim feeder. Black Cloud

has no smell or flavour but forms a very attractive cloud in the water. It breaks up beauti-
fully on the surface instead of going down
quickly and this makes it ideal for shallow, still
waters. Place several handfuls of Black Cloud
in a round bowl and add water a little at a
time. Mix the peat thoroughly with your fin-
gers and make sure that it forms balls when it
is squeezed. Once this happens, casters, corn
or chopped worms can be added. Black Cloud
is particularly attractive for big bream but it
also works on canals where tiny pinches can be
used on a regular basis. The slowly sinking
cloud attracts many fish eager for cover. Also,
as it contains no feed, they will not be overfed
and go off the hook-bait.

3 *Natural Baits*

One of the most satisfying ways of catching fish is to unlock their world and catch them as naturally as possible, on what they actually eat in the normal course of their lives. This skill needs a knowledge of the fish and their habitats and also keen powers of observation. For example, it is useful to be able to identify different weed types in the water which harbour specific forms of aquatic life. A great deal of natural bait fishing depends on opportunism. For example, a hatch of tadpoles or a wave of daddy-long-legs can both provoke a wild response from fish at particular times of the year.

A secondary benefit of natural baits is that they are either cheap or free, which is quite a bonus in an inflationary age when casters and boilies cost such serious money. The potential drawback is that in this over-used, abused world we might drain already endangered resources and life forms. For example, had this book been written thirty years ago, crayfish would certainly have figured largely in this particular chapter. Not now. Pollution and abstraction have hit stocks badly over the past decades and the use of survivors as bait would be quite irresponsible, apart from being illegal, and bring the justifiable wrath of conservation groups down on our heads. That does not mean, however, that there are not plentiful natural bait forms around. Some of them are possibly the best baits imaginable for the job.

FRESHWATER MUSSELS

Altogether there are over twenty different types of freshwater cockle and mussel in Britain but only one specimen is of any use to the anglers: the swan mussel (Fig. 3.1). This is a big mussel, often up to six inches in length, and is found in any unpolluted still water or flowing river in the country. It prefers to lie around the muddy shallows

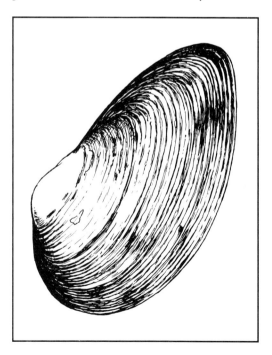

Fig. 3.1 A swan mussel.

especially near reeds or where overhanging trees create an umbrella of darkness. Mussels 'shoal' and move slowly around by means of a foot that comes out of the thick end of the two shells when they are held open. They feed by passing water through two tubes and retaining any particles of fine weed or small water-borne animals. They are very well camouflaged and their dark green or yellow shells blend in well with the fallen leaves on the bed.

The best place to look for swan mussels is where you can see shells open and broken, the remains of those caught by diving birds. It should then be a simple matter to rake out unopened shells or even to wade in and feel for them carefully in the soft mud. Half an hour's effort should see quite enough mussels gathered for a session's fishing. It used to be considered an advantage to open the shells (by means of a heavy knife) a day or two before fishing. The mussel would then smell rather rancid and this was considered important to attracting fish from afar. This, I feel, is something of an old fisherman's tale and I always prefer my mussels fresh.

In the heady specimen days of the 1960s and 1970s swan mussels were seen as a prime bait for tench, bream and carp. Through these years they were dredged out in vast quantities, opened up, chopped up and thrown back by legions of eager young men – myself included. They were quite a good bait, though not a magical one and they did catch bigger than average size fish. Their weight allowed them to be free-lined – a favourite method in those days – but setting the hook could be a problem. Great care was taken to ensure the hook point stood proud so that it would find flesh on the strike. Slivers of mussel were good, and perhaps the most popular piece was the bright yellow foot.

One of the great champions of the freshwater mussel in those early days was Frank Guttfield. He wrote first about its powers in *Angling* magazine way back in 1959:

'When you find a swim that contains a good bed of mussels do not drag any out of this swim but get them from another swim. Then use these mussels for hook-bait and fish with them in the swim where you know there is a good bed of mussels.

Tench and bream usually give determined bites with mussel, but if you are consistently getting knocks, try changing to a small hook and use small cubes of the bait instead.

When fishing at night and early morning, large lumps of mussel will usually prove the best, but the lighter it gets the more likely you are to take small fish on smaller cubes. Tench and bream are by no means the only fish that will take mussel. It is quite a good bait for perch, eels and even pike.'

There are things that could be added. For example, the shells are quite useful, especially if they are ground into small pieces and added to the groundbait bucket. They fall through the water and glitter like little scales and lie attractively on the bottom. Opening the shell can be very difficult and the best way is to hold the mussel firmly in one hand with the hinges of the shell facing towards you. Insert the knife along this join and gently cut the hinge. Both halves of the shell should then fall apart.

Swan mussels still exist in some numbers and cannot exactly be called rare. However, like so many things in the wild they have declined to a degree. Pollution and agricultural abstraction have affected many of their habitats and it is irresponsible to recommend their use as a bait totally unreservedly. Certainly the heavy prebaiting of the past should no longer be indulged in. Old writers regularly recommended forty or more mussels to be thrown into a swim before fishing commenced. Now, perhaps a single mussel used near to a bed is quite enough. There must be a case for a single mussel cast temptingly on to a ledge, right in the middle of a big tench's patrol route. This one-off approach could well land the fish of the season.

WOODLICE

For at least a century woodlice have been recognized as attractive baits for roach and dace. Last century, Greville Fennell, in his book on the roach, described particular situations when they were very effective on the Thames: 'To get on board a ship discharging timber was a great boon for there, the battens were thrust out of the porthole, countless woodlice would fall into the water and would attract shoals of fish which were only too eager for the coveted luxury to examine closely the baited hooks.'

I have not been tempted to use woodlice personally since childhood roach angling on Northern canals when they proved moderately successful. However, my own experiences count for little. That well-known Hampshire specimen hunter, Martin Hooper, wrote recently: 'I have caught barbel on many diverse baits including, would you believe, woodlice. You stick a hook in a woodlouse and see what it does: a good imitation of a large hempseed with legs, don't you think?'

Very recently, I tried woodlice myself for the most of a day. As Martin says, the hooked woodlouse does roll itself into something like a hempseed ball but I have got to say that hooking is very difficult indeed. The creature is surprisingly soft and tears quickly. Even more strange was the fact that though I was fishing a swim teaming with roach and rudd that took virtually everything I threw at them, the woodlouse would invariably hang unmolested for a long period of time. On a few occasions, a woodlouse was taken in the end but it was a long wait and really indicated to me that woodlice do perhaps have limited uses.

THE CADDIS

In the nineteenth century the caddis was a very popular and effective bait but it has fallen out of common usage simply through laziness. The caddis is not commercially available and usual modern-day anglers do not have the time, the energy or the inclination to hunt for baits themselves, however effective these may be.

In quicker streamy water, the caddis is the natural bait *par excellence*. Inevitably, many become dislodged and are swept down to the fish which must accept them as one of their most usual foodstuffs. Barbel, dace, chub and roach all accept caddis with great eagerness, especially on rivers where they have become used to treating anglers' baits with caution. The caddis is a larvae of the sedge fly. There are many different varieties but all of them look much alike. All of them make homes from underwater rubbish, dead water-weed stems, bits of twig, particles of gravel and sand, in fact anything that will glue together to make an impenetrable little house. Some caddis move around in these encasings searching for food and others remain anchored under stones or in reed and weed fronds. Eventually, the caddis will seal its mouth and, like a maggot, turn into a chrysalis from which the adult sedge fly hatches out on the surface.

Providing the water is pure, large numbers of caddis can be caught from shallow sections or where streams enter the main river. Wear polaroids and wade carefully, overturning stones and picking the caddis cases off the rocks where they are clinging. Any brick-sized stone will probably have half a dozen to a score of caddis clinging to it. If the caddis are to be used quickly, simply place them in an ordinary bait box with a good air flow. If, however, you are going to keep them for twenty-four hours or so, make sure there is plenty of damp grass or moss to keep them moist.

The type of swim where natural baits work well: shallow and streamy over gravel and weed.

To get the caddis from its case, gently nip the closed end and the alarmed caddis will pop out of the top. Grip it gently by the head and slide it smoothly from the case. Use a hook related to the size of the caddis and the species you are going to use it for. Generally hook sizes 12 to 16 are about right, the point slipping in gently through the tail.

In my experience, the caddis is best fished just off the bottom, under a float allowed to drift downstream to the waiting fish. This is probably how they expect caddis to reach them in the wild and takes are generally violent and positive, the float simply burying itself. Two or three caddis on a size 10 can be an effective barbel bait, especially when they are feeding on maggot and hemp but still retaining that customary wariness. As a summer roach bait, the caddis has few equals and it is a bait to sort out the very biggest dace in the river.

SILKWEED

From the summer onwards, underwater structures like weir sills, bridge supports, old pilings and large boulders in fast water are coated with thick bands of silkweed. This is a bright green weed with something like a cotton-wool texture. The weed is home to small shrimps and snails which provide an important food source for many species of fish. Fish either browse on the weed where it grows or wait for pieces to be washed down to them, especially in faster waters, and so it makes an excellent natural bait.

Silkweed fishing originally rose to prominence in the nineteenth century along the Thames. Many important anglers promoted its use for roach, dace, chub and even barbel. The use of silkweed spread to all the major river systems and its use became common around the turn of the century on the Trent, the Wessex rivers and the Severn.

One of the major problems in using silk-weed as a bait is putting the stuff on the hook. To pull tufts out by hand tends to crush the animal life that the weed contains. It's probably better to crop a patch with a rod rest and scoop it into a bait box half filled with water. Leave the lid off the bait box in warm weather otherwise the weed will stew and the special texture will be spoiled. The hook is baited by pulling it through the ball of weed in the bait box. It's best to fold strands round the shank a few times, otherwise the weed will tend to fall apart on the cast. The perfect hook size is a 10 or 12 and the weed is best fished under a float and trotted down the quick water where the fish expect to find clumps naturally.

Silkweed is rarely used these days and once again we have to wonder if there is any real merit in going to the extra trouble of

A little millpool like this is the perfect place to find silkweed.

collecting and using it. I know that John Wilson, the well-known Norfolk angler, is a great disciple of silkweed fishing and he surely knows a thing or two about roach fishing. I myself have used silkweed on the Norfolk millpools and found it moderately successful, though I have never decimated roach shoals in the way that the old writers suggest is possible using this 'miracle bait'. Once more, I feel its application is specialized. I would like to use it, perhaps, for that solitary big, wise chub that has seen every bait and tactic in the book and might just fall for a piece of weed carelessly brushing past its nose. On the Hampshire Avon, at the Royalty, I have seen barbel hoovering silkweed from the brickwork of the Parlour Pool. These fish have ignored all normal baits thrown at them so perhaps a clump of silkweed allowed to drift naturally through the shoal would attract attention.

SHRIMPS

Angling lore says that sea shrimps have attracted barbel, chub, perch and even tench after they have been boiled and peeled. Perhaps this is true but I have never personally met anybody who has used them.

The freshwater shrimp is a totally different prospect. This little crustacean, greyish in colour and growing to about half an inch long, is often gorged upon by chub and roach, especially when the weeds are being cut in the river in the summer and countless thousands of these little creatures are washed downstream. They are especially numerous in flannel weed, and a piece dragged out and examined on the bank will always reveal enough hook-baits for a long session.

A freshwater shrimp is perhaps best fished singly on a size 16 for roach or a clump on a size 10 or 12 could be used for chub or barbel. Dace, too, are also very responsive to a float-fished shrimp on a size 16 or 18 hook. In fact, float fishing is probably the best way to fish the shrimp as it is carried downriver in the most natural of ways by this method.

Again, the question must be asked whether the use of a shrimp is ever really necessary. The answer must be that in general terms it is not, but there must be occasions when an ultra-wary chub or roach will suck in something that seems to it entirely natural whereas it will reject an alien food source. I can think of examples in the past where a freshwater shrimp might well have proved irresistible to very cautious fish, had I possessed a little more breadth of imagination and daring.

CATERPILLARS

I suppose that any book on baits must include some mention of caterpillars though I am very unhappy to follow the trend that has been set in the past century. In today's high-pressured, highly farmed, highly polluted environment butterflies of all sorts are under severe threat and use of their grubs by anglers as bait for pure recreation seems to me to be indefensible. Very few anglers are experts on butterflies and it is quite possible that the caterpillars of rare species could unwittingly be used. On a more practical level, I am far from sure that caterpillars are in fact a truly useful bait. It is an old misconception that any caterpillar found along the river bank can be dapped into the mouth of some desperate chub. Undoubtedly fish will eat them at times but many caterpillars actually have a disgusting taste and smell and once they sense danger, often discharge noxious fluids through their skin. There is a very fair chance that the unwitting angler could therefore use a bait that his quarry finds absolutely repulsive.

Really, then, I think that I have said enough.

LOBWORMS, RED WORMS AND BRANDLINGS

Lobworms

Few anglers realize how many worms both river and stillwater fish eat during the average season. In times of flood, or heavy rain, countless thousands of lobs are washed into river systems from the surrounding fields and bank sides. When I owned a small half-acre pond, I found that a night thunderstorm would wash innumerable worms from the vegetable patch into the shallow margins where the carp were picking them up at dawn. Once, when the whole small valley flooded, a rough count of the shallows indicated several hundred, if not one thousand plus worms on their way into the pool.

In these stressful days of such limited time one of the largest problems with worm fishing is the very collecting of the bait. It is sometimes possible to buy lobworms from tackle dealers but the price is generally prohibitive and the really serious worm angler must rely on his own supplies. Probably the most common method is to 'snitch' worms at night. The 'Trent Otter' described this technique over eighty years ago in his book *Coarse Fish Angling* and his advice has never really been bettered:

'Worms can be picked up from May to October [*Author's note:* I personally believe any mild night throughout the winter is effective], but moonlight nights are not good, neither is it a certainty unless heavy rains or dews have fallen previously. Warm, muggy, dark nights are preferable. I have picked up many thousands. You can see them stretched out on the grass with just a small portion of their tails in their holes, and so sensitive are they that a light footfall causes them to disappear in an instant. Extreme caution must mark the movements of a "worm dodger" or he will not get one fourth of those he sees stretched out; he must have a bag with a wide open mouth hung round his neck, a lantern or lamp in his left hand so that the light hits the ground directly in front of him; with the right

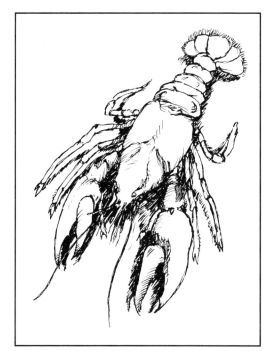

Fig. 3.2 Crayfish.

Brandlings are excellent for bream, tench and carp.

he carefully grips the worm below the band near the centre and a steady pull brings it out. Some nights the worms are so very sensitive to vibration – there may be plenty in reach – the slightest movement of foot or hand causes them to vanish instantly. I have had to work a couple of hours to get as many hundreds, while on the other hand certain nights and certain conditions of weather have resulted in one or two thousand being collected in the same time.

Expert worm catchers are so clever at it they will pick them out of the grass in an instant and so careful are they that not more than a dozen bruised or crushed worms will be found in a thousand of their catching. This is one of the things that the novice must be cautioned in: don't bruise or pinch your worms, as fifty crushed worms in your scouring tubs will speedily ruin the lot.'

Worm hunting is a job that is well done in the closed season when fishing is not a distraction. Many hundreds of worms can be collected long before June and the big question is how to store them. Martin Hooper suggests:

'The most useful thing for the job is a plastic tank. The sort that you have in the loft is ideal but I don't suggest that you use it. Demolition sites are the places to get one or two for next to nothing. Once you have acquired a tank, drill a couple of dozen holes along the underside of the tank. Place four inches of fine gravel in the bottom of the tank, over this place layers of newspaper, then a mixture of finely sieved soil, moss and shredded newspaper. The gravel is to allow for drainage and stops a lot of the worms from entering the bottom of the tank and then escaping via the drainage holes. After collection spread the worms out on the top of the soil mixture and leave well alone until the morning. Any

worms that have not then gone down into the tank must be removed even if nothing appears wrong with them. As with the proverb, one bad apple spoils the bunch and so does one bad worm.

In times of dry weather, water the soil well. Turn the soil frequently with a fork and remove any suspect worms. This also serves to harden the worms up by forcing them to work a lot harder than they would normally. It is useful to place a few turfs on top of the soil as these will stop the tank drying out too quickly and also feed the worms. Around once a month remove half the soil and replace with fresh to avoid bacteria from accumulating. Any worms left from a fishing trip should be treated as if you had just collected them and placed on top of the soil or turf to be discarded the following morning if necessary. Often worms will start to breed in the tank and these will grow on if left and supplement your supply for the season.'

The other alternative is to create a wormery in a shaded part of the garden. This need not be too large, say around two yards square. Simply knock some stakes into the soil and fence the area in with planks. Dig the bottom out around twelve inches and lay a four or five inch layer of loose gravel to provide drainage. It is then simply a job of filling this pen with manure, rotting compost and all manner of kitchen waste especially orange peel, potato skins, lettuce leaves, pea shells and the like. Tea leaves are supposed to be especially nutritious. Over the top, mole-hill soil can be placed and on top of that some old turfs, again to keep in moisture. As with Martin Hooper's tank, put collective worms on top of the wormery and allow them to burrow their own way in. Any that are too sick to accomplish this again must be discarded. In very dry weather it pays to water the wormery quite frequently but not to soak it. Damp

Proof that worms do work.

Country men know a couple of old tricks to collect worms. One is to put a long fork into an attractive-looking piece of soil and wiggle it furiously from side to side. The principle is that the worms, presumably confused, will rise to the surface in bewilderment where they can be picked up and put in the box. I have seen this happen so I do know that it does work. The second trick is to pour a gallon of soapy water over a piece of soil. The worms presumably do not like the soap and come to the surface in order to get away from it. Again, it is a simple matter to dig up the dejected little creatures.

Transporting the worms to the waterside has always been a matter of deep discussion, with many anglers over the years having their own favourite techniques. Traditionally, a bucket filled with sphagnum moss (available from florists) has been used. The idea is that the moss cleans and toughens the worms as they go through it. This seems to be an awful lot of trouble to me and I am not at all sure whether the lobworm particularly needs any toughening anyway. Its skin is generally like rhino hide and to toughen it further would probably put many a fish off. The method might have some use for brandlings and red worms which are softer and can break on the hook. The old writer 'Faddist' recommended that the worms should be kept in fine sand or even brick dust with a view to reddening their skins – altogether too inhuman a treatment for me! As for myself, I found the important thing is to give the worms plenty of air. This is why I do not use the normal bait box but much prefer a bucket filled with a little moist soil, some wet grass and perhaps a few old lettuce leaves. In such a container worms should live very happily for a couple of days, quite long enough for the normal fishing expedition. Naturally, if the weather is particularly hot and bright it pays to keep the bucket in the shade or under a cloth.

sacks or cloths can also be laid over to keep in the moisture and keep off the heat of the burning sun. In an ideal wormery, the inhabitants will breed very quickly indeed. Lobworms are slower but brandlings and red worms can reproduce faster than hamsters! A good wormery can be kept going for years especially if the compost and kitchen waste is regularly replenished and a fresh breeding stock of worms added from time to time. A good wormery will provide all your bait needs for a very long time indeed.

However, not everyone has a garden or has the time to create and look after a wormery. A few dozen worms for a one-off fishing trip can also simply be dug from the ground. Certain places hold more than others. Damp areas under trees are particularly good, especially if the soil has not been turned for some time. A particular favourite of mine is the area round an old septic tank – niffy but prolific. Road drainage ditches are also excellent. The areas around compost heaps or field margins, especially hard under the hedgerows, are often very good.

If the physical act of digging does not appeal, a quiet word with the farmer might give you the permission to follow the plough at certain times of the year and fight for the worm along with the accompanying seagulls.

A lovely crucian carp that fell to worm.

The lobworm is probably my own favourite natural bait and I like to use it whole for chub, barbel, carp, tench, bream, perch, eels, and even roach and rudd. The best worm to use is a live one, so barbed hooks are generally necessary to prevent the worm from wriggling off. With a big lobworm, on, say, a size 4 or size 6 hook it is quite enough to pass the point a couple of times through the body, and the worm will still wriggle attractively (Fig. 3.3). However, normally, I like to pass a worm just once through the middle. All worms have what is called a saddle, a large band on their bodies. Through experience I have found that it is best to put the hook above this saddle – towards the head – otherwise the worm tends to die much more quickly. Possibly what vital organs a worm possess are beneath this point.

Some people prefer to thread the worm on to the hook. This I have found quite unnecessary, messy and kills the worm quickly. Another old technique was to use a large lobworm on a double-hook rig. This I have tried years ago and now detest. The fear is that the fish will be hooked on one of the hooks and the second one will be free to do what damage it likes to the eye or gill flaps.

Chopped lobworms make an excellent groundbait. A medium to large lob can be cut into about ten half-inch portions. Fifty or so pieces introduced roughly every half an hour should keep even a large group of tench interested. Even when the worms themselves have gone there is still the lingering aroma of the juices in the water. Lobworm pieces can also be mixed with maggots or hemp to provide

Right: A lovely Wye barbel.

Below: A small maggot-caught rudd.

A pretty summer dace.

A superb carp for Danish expert Johnny Jensen.

A good Scottish fish.

A big brown trout next to a lure box.

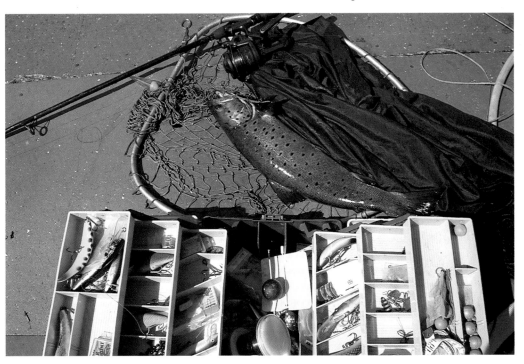

Above: A river rich in natural food.

Below: A vast array of boilies.

Right: The late, great John Sidley with a big eel caught on dead bait.

Julian Cundiff with a large spring twenty.

Left: Modern groundbait being mixed.

Below: A wasp nest ready for the freezer.

A freezing winter's day – choice of bait is critical.

A good-looking carp taken on traditional bait.

Chub on a slug caught by the author.

very attractive carpets of food for most species. When mixed with groundbait, worm pieces do have the tendency to make the balls disintegrate in the air. For this reason it pays to mix a groundbait a little stiffer than usual and this in itself can be a problem in shallow, clear water with suspicious, easily spooked fish.

In particularly weedy waters, worms can hide themselves from a fish very effectively within a few minutes. One way of overcoming this is to nip a quarter of an inch off each end of the worm. Maimed in this way the worm finds it impossible to burrow. Another alternative is to use three drowned worms. Though this does sound ghastly, the method is effective. I have heard it said and indeed read it many times that a dead worm is repulsive to fish. This is nonsense providing the worm has not been long dead, and I suspect that some fish will take a dead worm in preference to a live one. The third method of presenting a lobworm over a weedy bottom is to inject it with air to give it buoyancy and lift it out of harm's way. Of course, using a syringe

A brandling sweetcorn cocktail often works wonders.

is a dangerous business and great care must be taken not to inject air into one's own finger.

Red Worms

Red worms are short, slim, firm fleshed and coloured quite vividly. They make a superb bream bait on all water types and can be fished in conjunction with maggots, casters and hemp. They are also superb for tench, roach, barbel and in small bunches for carp.

Fig. 3.3 Worms on the hook.

Brandlings

Brandlings are almost equally as good as red worms and can be found in vast quantities in most compost heaps or amongst the refuse in pig farms. Brandlings have yellowish bands on their dark red bodies; they frequently don't look particularly well and so seem to die and stretch faster than other worms. Perhaps this is the one worm type that does benefit in a moss-filled bucket. Once again, every fish species finds brandling most acceptable and they are particularly useful for finicky crucian carp on a day when bread and maggots are rejected.

BLOODWORM

The bloodworm is the larva of the gnat. It is generally found in lakes and ponds where some degree of pollution exists. A typical example would be a farm pond which is polluted by animal manure. Bloodworms are rare in rivers though they can occasionally be found in stagnant, slack sections. They are small, fragile, bright red worms that spend their lives in the bottom silt and mud, feeding off pieces of debris. Small fish such as gudgeon obviously feed a great deal on these worms and, for this reason, the bloodworm became a favourite bait of the northern canal angler. However, wherever bloodworm exist in numbers, fish of all sorts will feed heavily upon them, and the use of bloodworm as a bait should therefore have a wider scope.

Bloodworm are often used in conjunction with the joker. The joker is the larva of the midge. In appearance it is simply a miniature bloodworm. Jokers are only found in running water that is most definitely polluted. The best kind of joker water is a stream which receives sewage effluent. Wherever there is a sewage works discharging into a stream or river there will always be jokers present. However, from April to June they tend to be in short supply because this is when the insects' reproductive cycle is at its peak – fortunately coinciding with the coarse fish closed season.

The life cycles of bloodworm and jokers are rather similar. The gnat, or midge, lay its eggs on the water's surface rather like a fly will blow its eggs on to offal or fish. These eggs sink to the bed where the bloodworms (or jokers) will hatch out. They remain in the silt until the water begins to warm sometime around April. In the same way as a maggot develops a chrysalis, the bloodworm also changes, developing a white lump on its head. This grows until the head is twice its normal size and then it floats to the surface where the gnat or midge bursts free out of the head itself. The discarded body is left on the lake surface, a clue to the existence of bloodworm beneath. In fact, on some waters these 'shuks' or 'casts' are so thick that they clog the line and make fishing almost impossible. The midges and gnats hatch throughout the summer and activity only grows quiet again as the water begins to cool.

For either the pleasure fisherman or the match fisherman bloodworm offer a great opportunity and the way to fish them is described by Dave Roper, perhaps the leading exponent of this method:

'The first job is to obtain the bait. It is possible to buy bloodworm from some tackle shops or direct from professional gatherers – and, in fact, to start with it might be an idea to go fishing with shop-bought worms – but I feel anyone wanting to win a match with this bait must be prepared to collect it himself for the fresher it is the better it works. If there is a secret to bloodworm, that is it.

I always collect my bait on the morning of the match, and, while it often means getting out of bed very early, the effort is worth while.

Bloodworm are found all over England, in lakes and ponds. Unfortunately there is no common factor to the type of water and conditions in which they are found, so the only sensible advice, is to buy a map and go out and check all the waters shown.

There is no short cut. I once spent a week's holiday doing nothing but visiting ponds and lakes shown on a local map. The result, after trudging over dozens of fields, was three workable waters containing sufficient bloodworm to make scraping viable.

The most likely waters are those with a stream running in and out – especially if they carry minor pollution such as from a pond. Small farm ponds used regularly by cattle are well worth trying because they help create the right conditions. One thing all the ponds must have is mud.

It is necessary to get into the water to collect the bait, which obviously means the pond must be reasonably shallow. And it naturally follows that waders are essential; chest-waders are best of all but don't rush out and buy them until you are sure bloodworm is going to fit into your fishing plans on a regular basis.

The traditional and most efficient method of gathering bloodworm is with a scraper. These are easily made and consist of a stainless-steel blade one inch wide and one-sixteenth of an inch thick. The blade would be about eighteen inches long and fixed at right-angles to some sort of wooden shaft; and it's worth making the handle long enough to act as a wading stick.

Although collecting bloodworm is called "scraping", the actual action of passing the blade through the mud should be done

Quiver-tipping a worm at dusk for a chub.

smoothly – similar to the way in which a golfer uses a putter. The scraper is passed gently under the mud and lifted out at the end of each stroke. If bloodworm are present they will be brought out on the leading edge of the blade.

The next step is to place the worms in a container. The cheapest method is to use a ladies' nylon stocking, which can be fitted with tape or string and hung about your neck, so as to leave the hands free while in the water. The worms are simply pushed from the blade into the stocking. The bait can be cleaned later by dousing the stocking in the water to remove excess mud.

Anglers who collect a lot of bloodworm use two floating trays fitted with fine mesh and designed so that one fits inside the other. The top tray has a relatively large mesh, which allows the worms to pass through but removes the larger debris. The finer mesh of the second tray permits only the mud and silt to wash away, leaving the worms reasonably clean. With luck we will have now reached the stage where there are enough worms for a day's fishing – two pints of neat worms will be more than enough for most venues.

All I do now is place the worms in a folded newspaper to dry them off, and that is how I take them to the fishing match. They will keep in newspaper for a day or more – but do remember that the fresher the bait the better.

I seldom use the smaller worms, known as jokers, and honestly think it would be a waste of time discussing them in any depth. Suffice to say they are usually found in running water such as land drains and the methods of collecting them are the same. To my mind jokers are unnecessary for catching bigger fish, and bloodworm is ample on its own.

There are no secrets to collecting or fishing with bloodworm; once you become involved it is easy. Don't listen to the involved stories concerning them (most are invented by ill-informed people), just have faith in my methods to begin with, then adapt them to suit your own style and, if you wish, go on to experiment further.

Fishing Bloodworm

A mystique surrounds bloodworm fishing which tends to make anglers believe that specialized tackle is needed – that's a load of rubbish. I could go to a child fishing on the local canal with maggot or caster and, after showing him how to put a bloodworm on the hook, he would catch fish without changing his gear at all!

I can extend the theme to explode some other myths. For instance, I never use the peat-based groundbait known as "black", barbless hooks are more of a hindrance when bloodworm fishing, and it is not essential to use Continental tackle and bristle floats. So there is nothing to prevent any reader buying or collecting a pint of bloodworm today, then going along to his favourite water with normal tackle and catching fish – it's as straightforward as that. Having been brought up to accept bloodworm as a normal part of angling, I have naturally developed a style when using it. And basically it is to fish as fine as conditions allow. Nowadays I prefer a roach-pole and the lighter tackle that goes with it. The pole makes for precision fishing, whether I have maggot, caster or bloodworm on the hook. I will happily fish with bloodworm on normal rod and line, and if conditions dictate I use it when legering. I must stress it is normal bait and all normal tackle rules apply.

The hooks I use for bloodworm are Mustad 313 – a fine-wire pattern with a barb – and I usually work between sizes 24 and 20. Barbless hooks can be used but fresh bloodworm can be so lively that they will swim off the hook, and in match fishing that would be a waste of time to say the least.

Care must be taken when putting the worm on the hook. They are frail creatures and should be hooked lightly through the head. If you place the hook in any part other than the top section, the worm will burst and the red fluid escape, leaving an empty case.

My line breaking strain varies depending upon where I am fishing and what size of fish I expect. The lightest line is 12oz but I'm just as likely to use 1lb or 1½lb breaking strain.

When it comes to lead shot I am still a fan of the normal round split lead but occasionally use olivettes on pole tackle to get the bait down quickly in deep water. The important point is to place the shot on the line in the correct position   and that's no different whatever the bait. The same rules apply to the floats. If I'm using a roach-pole under good conditions, I will probably choose a bristle-tipped pattern carrying a couple of small shot. Then again, if I need to cast farther with running line the float might be a loaded peacock waggler. Really, the actual tackle doesn't matter, provided it is sensible and put together correctly. There is no special float, hook or lead shot designed solely for use with blood-worm.

When it comes actually to fishing there are many variations on how to introduce the bloodworm into the swim and most of them seem to involve "black". Black is a peat or soil-based groundbait used either on its own to form a cloud, or with additives such as sand to make it sink more quickly. I never use it, and feel it is one of the areas that confuse some anglers and make them shy away from fishing with bloodworm. It has reached the stage now where people are looking for exotic additives such as bird-droppings to mix with their groundbait, but surely if these things were so good it wouldn't be necessary to introduce bloodworm! The truth is that the fish come for the bloodworm.

I prefer to think of the worms as I would maggots, and basically put them into the swim in the same manner. When fishing a shallow still water or canal – say when the water is no deeper than four feet – I loose-feed the blood-worm. On deeper water I use breadcrumb and, to help bind it together, I add powdered clay. The clay helps to bind the bread-feed and actual amounts will depend on conditions. The groundbait is mixed with a sprinkling of water in the normal manner. There is no reason why bread-feed could not be used on its own – after all it's there to do a job, and that's to get the worms down to the fish.

The size of the hook-bait must be matched to the size of fish; it might be a single worm for small roach and perch, or three or four bloodworm on the hook for skimmers and larger bream.

I am a firm believer that the best place to make a good catch is the canal or lake bottom, and on most occasions I will concentrate on that area by setting the tackle to trip bottom or laying-on. The exception are perch. They are mainly midwater feeders and so I set my tackle to fish on-the-drop and keep the shoal up in the water by feeding little and often.

I have covered everything needed to get started on bloodworm fishing. I'm sure I could have made the whole business sound complicated, but it isn't and there is no big deal connected with bloodworm. It is just another method – but a good one!'

SLUGS

The writings of anglers past suggest that bream, carp, tench and barbel can all be caught on slugs. Perhaps they can on rare occasions. What is in no doubt, however, is that chub do very readily accept these rather repulsive-looking creatures. Three types of slug, the red, the black and the great grey,

Little can beat a big black slug for a chub.

seem to be the most effective. These are big slugs and sitting on a size 4 or 6 hook are a very attractive alternative to the normal chub bait. They're effective float fished, legered or freelined. Chub appear to like their taste and certainly just the very splash of a heavy three- or four-inch slug hitting the water will attract any chub in the area. There are, of course, no miracle baits but certainly a large juicy slug on a grey damp morning in the late summer seems nearly to fit the bill.

It is possible to collect slugs and keep them long term in an aquarium filled with garden soil and fed on household waste, green-grocery and grass cuttings. All this seems rather too much bother to me, especially for an occasional bait. Most of the slugs even the ardent chub angler is likely to need can be found around compost heaps, particularly after dark. However, on most moist, mild nights, the pathway around fields and in gardens are strewn with slow-moving slugs that are very easy to catch. It is a simple matter to put these in a normal bait box with grass and perhaps even the odd lettuce leaf.

Among 'slug men' over the decades there has been some rivalry, not in catching the biggest chub but in breeding the biggest slug! Apparently these creatures adore melons and if a hole is bored in the tough outside skin the slugs will force their way in and eat the entire inner contents. Such gorging on nutritious food grows enormous baits and slugs of five, six and even a massive reputed seven inches are possible. I suppose, then, the only task is finding a chub big enough to eat it.

WASP GRUBS

According to my diaries, it was in 1956 that I first made the attempt to fish with a wasp grub. I had located a nest in a neighbour's garden and set about digging it out one afternoon in mid-August. It shows my tenacity that I only conceded defeat after having collected a total of thirty-seven stings and not a single grub! Fortunately, there are safer ways to proceed. Finding a nest should not be too difficult. It is important to watch the wasps that are flying quickly in a straight line, preferably holding items of food if you can see these. These are the workers, flying back to their nest with provisions. Follow such a wasp for as far as you can until you lose it or some 'obstruction gets in your way. Simply wait until the next straight-flying wasp comes along and follow that, too, as far as you can. It is not often that you need to follow more than four or five wasps before finding their nest in a bank, a tree or an old wall.

The wasp nest at dawn when all is quiet.

Chemists or in particular garden stores sell the types of poison needed to exterminate nests. Spread it before sunset, allow a couple of hours for the poison to work and then begin to dig. Make sure at this stage that you are very adequately clothed because, although most of the wasps will be dead, there might be a few still groggily alive. Remember, too, that dead wasps can still administer a sting so wear thick gardening gloves at this stage. Take the nests out whole, put them into polythene bags and then slip the whole lot into the freezer at home.

There are endless ways of using the grubs and the cake they live in as bait. Do, however, remember that the grubs are very soft and do not stand up to long casting in the way of maggots. Fished close in, quite gently, wasp grubs make a superb bait for chub, barbel, tench, carp, roach, rudd, crucian carp and perch. In fact, there are very few British coarse fish that can resist a succulent wasp grub!

Spraying the wasp nest with poison.

Next morning, removing the defunct wasp nest. Notice that gloves are worn.

The tools and the result.

The cake is excellent broken up and allowed to drift down the current. It can be fished exactly like floating crust for chub and is a very useful alternative when they get suspicious of that particular bait. In fact, even if they continue to be wary, their greed for the succulent cake generally gets the better of them.

The cake can also be used mashed up in groundbait or even in a swimfeeder. There is something about the smell of it that drives most fish species wild and can provoke the most violent feeding spells. In fact, during the 1970s at least, I do know of the bait being banned from several matches simply because it was said to give the competitor an unfair edge.

A dead wasp in itself can make an excellent bait for chub. This is particularly so in September when the adults tend to gorge themselves on the sap of trees, become groggy and fall into the margins. Chub soon learn to accept these titbits without any of their usual suspicion. Dapping, that much neglected art, is that way to present a dead wasp. You need a long rod, a suitably sized hook and the ability to creep and crawl through the undergrowth. Let the baited hook dangle on a short length of line from the rod tip over the swim. Inch your way towards where the chub is waiting and slowly lower the bait to the waiting fish. You'll be amazed how the chub react to the sight of a dead wasp dropping from the heavens. The slower the descent, the more frenzied the chub appears, sometimes actually boiling on the surface in its eagerness. As the bait touches the water drop the rod tip and the chub will engulf it violently. Have the clutch of the reel set quite loose or a line break is virtually inevitable.

Finally, let me repeat that it is the lazy man who does not want to try wasp grubs and the foolish man who overlooks the potential dangers. Do check with your chemist about all the safety precautions relating to the poison chosen. Do wait until darkness before attacking the nest and do wear ample protective clothing. Take no risks either with the chemical or the insect itself. No fish is worth the discomfort that I suffered nearly forty years ago.

A piece of reed caught a grass carp.

4 *Modern Developments*

The carp scene since 1960 has absolutely exploded on us all. There are more carp, more carp waters and more carp anglers and, as a result, competition and knowledge have increased many fold. Tackle has become very important and so have rigs but probably it is in the area of baits that most research has been done. Thirty years ago, no angler would have heard of boilies, floaters or even particles. These are new concepts to be explained in depth.

BOILED BAITS
by Julian Cundiff

It's funny how just one bait can be viewed in so many different ways by anglers today. To non-carp anglers, talk of boiled baits, or boilies as they are more commonly known, brings to mind weird-smelling little round things that can ruin fishing for general anglers. However, mention boilies to the carp anglers and you will start an endless discussion on fishmeal or bird seed, protein or semolina, maple or cherry. A bit like a favourite float, everybody has a favourite boilie and yet we all still experiment with new ones each season.

So what is a boilie and what are all these technical terms carp anglers talk about nowadays? Well a boilie is, as its name suggests, an item that has been boiled in water to give it a hard skin. Usually, it consists of dry powder added to eggs and flavour, mixed into a paste, rolled into balls, boiled and fed to the carp. Easy, isn't it?

While boilies have been around a long time, they only became truly popular in the early to mid-1980s when carp angling took off in a big way. Books such as *Carp Fever* and *The Carp Strikes Back* dispelled the myths of carp fishing as a secret society, and within these books were contained stories and secrets to inspire many anglers to take up carp fishing. Recipes which had caught and, probably more importantly, still did catch carp were printed in full and now all carp anglers would have an equal chance of catching those illusive specimens. In a short period of time, baits became commercially available and by 1984 you didn't even have to make your own boilies as Richworth actually sold them, ready rolled and ready to fish with. Now that the 1990s are upon us, the boilie boom has really taken over and at the last count there were thirty-seven different companies in England alone selling boilies. Unfortunately, with progress has come confusion: article after article, pamphlet after pamphlet full of intricate recipes and weird-sounding concoctions have only served to confuse today's angler, rather than educate or inform. So, in this chapter I will look at types of boilie, how to make your own boilies and one or two little tricks that catch that favourite species of ours – the carp.

Boilies were intended for fish like these.

Firstly, why do boilies work? Well, we all know carp are inquisitive creatures (as are most species). They will investigate anything that they find in their watery kingdom and when that item resembles food it will be sampled and usually eaten. If you ever watch small fish in an aquarium you will see them suck up stones, weed and all sorts of rubbish from the bottom of the tank. To a carp a boilie is just another food item like a snail, worm or piece of flake. It will pick it up, either eat it or blow it out and hopefully one day pick one up with a hook in it. So don't think for one moment boilies are mystical, magical items that drug the carp; they are food items in the long food chain of the fish. If they are made readily available and are acceptable, they will become a major food item and will be taken readily while the carp chew that form of food. To a certain extent, carp can almost be weaned on to boilies, but a good hatch of snails, bloodworms or larvae will soon tempt the carp back to its natural food sources. So don't get confused by all the waffle you read. You are offering the fish a food item, and it will choose it if it wants it.

Having discussed why carp eat boilies, now let's look at the different types of boilie there are, and how to choose the one that will suit your fishing best. Just as there are different styles of angling to catch carp, there are different forms of boilies to catch carp as well. There is no wonder recipe of 3oz of this, 3oz of that and 2fl oz of good luck – and thank goodness, too! Wouldn't it be horrible if we found an irresistible bait? All the excitement

A Welsh wildie that in this instance took bread.

would be taken out of our sport. So don't for one minute think that one day you will have the perfect boilie. You won't, because it does not exist.

As we said earlier, boilies consist of dry powder (the base mix) mixed with eggs (or water) and flavour. It is the dry-mix part that determines what kind of boilie you will have. Generally, the dry-mix part consists of milk powders such as casein, egg albumin, lactallumin, which when mixed with the eggs and boiled, form your bait. However, by varying what goes into the dry mix we can change what kind of a boilie it is. For most carp anglers, there are five main types of boilie.

a) **Fishmeal** A high percentage of the dry powder is made up from fishmeal ingredients such as capelin, herring meal, tuna meal, etc. Mixed with milk powders and such like, this is very nutritious to the carp and has been very successful in the last couple of years.

b) **Birdseed** Here a high percentage of the bait comprises birdseed ingredients such as robin red, or sluice, etc. These, too, are very attractive to carp and can be very successful.

c) **High protein** In this mix the dry powder has a very high protein rating and tends to be of very good-quality milk powders. If you believe that carp will pick out the best food to feed on this should be the best bait. However, its price and the fact that the carp will eat most food items tend to cast doubt on that theory.

d) **Low protein** Here the dry powder is of a cheaper nature with not as high a protein level. Ingredients such as semolina and soya powder on their own may not be overly attractive to carp but, when mixed with good flavours, many anglers do catch a lot of good fish on them.

e) **Mixed baits** This is where you combine two types of base mix to get a combination bait. You could cross fishmeal and bird seed, or protein and bird seed, or whatever, to give the carp the best of both worlds. Again, these types have been very successful.

So these are the types of boilie you can choose. Now what forms can you buy them in? Well, as before, progress has been a boon to the carp angler and you can choose your boilies in three different forms: ready rolled, base mixes and dry powder.

The simplest way to get boilies is, of course, to purchase ready-made ones. Firms such as Streamselect, Crafty Catcher and Zenon Bojko have taken the hard work out of it for you and have huge ranges for today's carp angler. These vary in size from 8mm–22mm and come in all colours, flavours, textures – the lot. You can even choose boilies for the freezer or ones you can just leave in your rucksack (shelf life) to use as and when needed. The obvious advantages of such ready-made boilies are that all the hard work is done for you in advance and that the baits are absolutely round. Also, generally, the boilie has been tried for at least a year in advance and has caught well. The disadvantages are that they tend to cost a little more, sometimes are not quite as good quality as your own mixes and you don't really have too much idea about what has gone into them. However, for those new to carp fishing, they are ideal.

The second form of boilie is where you purchase a base mix from the firm. All you need to do is add eggs, flavour, then boil, and catch! Again, this type of boilie is very popular today, possibly the most popular. A large

Carp go wild for boilies on a shelf.

number of firms offer all types of bird seed, protein and fishmeal mixes for you to play about with. Generally, these mixes are available in one-pound or three-pound bags and come with a sheet of suggested recipes, so provided you keep to the right amount of eggs and boiling times, you can add your favourite flavours or whatever. These types of base mix are very popular as they do provide you with a good catching base and the choice of flavour, colour and size is still left to you. The disadvantage, of course, is that you have to do all the hard work of rolling them yourself and some of these flavours don't half make your kitchen stink!

Our final form, the pure ingredients, used to be your only choice in the late 1970s but

Some of the flavours now available.

now very few people choose this form. Here you have to concoct recipes of so many ounces of this, so many ounces of that and find a base mix that not only mixes up well but boils well and then actually catches fish! Obviously, if you have a good recipe it is worth doing but unless you do have one, steer well clear of following such a course of action. For every dry mix that does work well there have been hundreds that haven't even got past the mixing stage. You have been warned!

Now we've seen the types and forms you can get boilies in, let's take a brief look at how to make these boilies from scratch. Obviously, with ready-mades, all you need to do is open the pack and away you go! With base mixes and dry ingredients you are going to need to combine dry powder with binder (eggs, etc.) to form a paste. Now that sounds easy, usually is easy, but can be an awfully messy and expensive chore if you don't get it right. So here is a step-by-step guide to doing it properly.

1 Crack whatever amount of eggs you need (*see* recipe below) into a large bowl and beat thoroughly until a yellow liquid is present.
2 Add to this your flavour, colour and any other liquid compounds and again stir vigorously.

3 Put your dry base mix into a freezer bag and give it a good one-minute shake to make sure all the dry ingredients are mixed together properly.
4 Gradually add the dry mix to the eggs, part stirring with a strong fork until a reasonable paste is formed.
5 Take the paste in your hands and keep kneading it in the large bowl, putting in more base mix until a nice firmish paste is achieved. As long as the dough is not sticking to your hands and is not cracking, it is properly mixed.
6 Break a lump off and, using a Gardner rolling table, roll out a sausage. Keep doing this until all your mixture is rolled into sausages.
7 Once you've rolled all your sausages, put them separately on a Gardner rollaball and roll out into round balls. Obviously, you don't need to roll them into balls if you are fishing at short range as you can chop the paste up into all shapes.
8 Put up to twenty baits at a time (18mm ones) in a pan of boiling water and boil for the recommended time. This will usually appear on the base mix recipe and can vary between 1–3 minutes.
9 Once the boiling period is reached, whip them out and put them on a nice absorbent towel to dry (preferably overnight).
10 Freeze them or take them to the lake.

So there you have it – a step-by-step guide to making your own boilies. You don't have to make your own boilies, as many of the country's most famous carp anglers will testify. Anglers such as Ritchie Macdonald, Andy Little, Peter Springate and Chris Ball only use ready-made baits and all four are very successful anglers. Do what you think is best and not what some expert from a hundred miles away tells you to do. Quite literally, there are hundreds of different base mixes, flavours and recipes for carp anglers today. In just one chapter we could not hope to cover everything on boilies but let us end with a list of my favourite recipes that have caught me a lot of carp from three to thirty pounds and will catch you just as many.

Recipe 1 – Low Protein Mix
16oz Nutramix (Nutrabaits)
4 Large size 2 eggs
3ml Cranberry Nutrafruit (Nutrabaits)
1ml Intense sweetener (Nutrabaits)
Colour red
Boil 2 minutes.

Recipe 2 – Yellow Bird Seed Mix
16oz Enervite Gold (Nutrabaits)
4 Large size 2 eggs
3ml SBS Cornish Ice Cream (SBS)
1½ml SBS Strawberry Jam (SBS)
2 Level teaspoons Milk 'B' (Cotswold Baits)
No colour
Boil 90 seconds.

Recipe 3 – Red Bird Seed Mix
20oz Big Fish Mix (Nutrabaits)
6 Large size 2 eggs
30ml Nutramine (Nutrabaits)
30ml Salmon Oil (Nutrabaits)
4ml Tutti-Frutti Nutrafruit (Nutrabaits)
No colour
Boil 90 seconds.

Finally, you will hear a lot of rubbish talked about bait so don't get confused. All the above recipes will catch you and me plenty of carp so you can be equally as confident with them as I am. Should anybody wish to know anything about specific recipes for baits then feel free to write to me: Julian Cundiff, 37 Oaklands, Camblesforth, Selby, North Yorks. YO8 8HH, enclosing a large SAE for a reply.

Good fishing.

Pop-up and Mini-Boilies

Over recent years 'pop-up' boilies have become very popular. There are two concepts involved here. Firstly, a pop-up can mean that the boilie is suspended anywhere from just below the surface to just above the bottom. Generally, however, they are set to float two, three or four inches from the bed, although a midwater boilie does catch fish. Fished in this way, the 'pop-up' is very much a novelty bait. The carp sees it quickly, makes a decision and hopefully is hooked. The problem is, of course, that pop-ups have a fairly short life and the carp soon wise up to what is a blatantly obvious technique.

The second, less fully understood, concept of the pop-up is more of a balanced bait. The philosophy is that the boilie is made to some extent buoyant so that it counterbalances the weight of the hook. Therefore, when carp come into the swim and begin to feed over a bed of boilies, the hooked boilie behaves exactly like the unhooked article. Thus, a carp that sucks at a balanced boilie will find that it floats into its mouth with just the same ease as one not attached to a hook or line. Also, when the carp are feeding avidly, they stir the boilies up with their fins and then turn round and take them when they are often a little way off the bottom. The balanced boilie behaves perfectly in this respect and is easily swirled from the bed of the lake.

Both pop-up and balanced boilies are easily created by using the Marvic Boilie Punch. This is an ingenious tool designed by Scott Coe for excavating a piece from the boilie which can be filled with foam to make it buoyant. The hole is then plugged over the foam so that the carp see no difference whatsoever. The tool is easy to use, is cheap and has become one of the best-selling products on the carp market. Indeed, many carpers find it an essential tool and it is certainly an easier

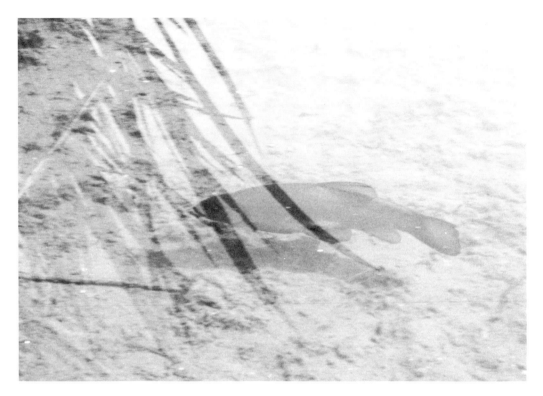

Mini-boilies work for tench in crystal-clear water.

way of creating a buoyant boilie than messing about with base mixes or microwaving.

At this point, it is worth mentioning mini-boilies. As the name suggests, these are simply boilies made small so that they look rather like a particle bait. Indeed, mini-boilies are a cross between boilies proper and particles and in many cases deliver the best of both worlds. 'Minis' are excellent for carp but work equally well for tench, bream, barbel, roach and even rudd. They are fished in much the same way as any other larger particle and can themselves be made buoyant, or at least balanced, by tying a middy polystyrene ball behind them. It is even possible, if one is prepared to do a very fiddly job, to excavate a mini-boilie and insert one of the polystyrene balls inside.

FLOATING BAITS

The concept of floating baits for rudd, chub, as well as carp is an old one. Very early writers realized that rudd and chub were quite happy to feed off the surface and methods were designed to capitalize on this. Today, it is carp and float fishing that are synonymous – a result of developments that began before World War II. Indeed, it is common to think that floating crust fishing really began with Walker but as BB's *Fisherman Bedside Book* makes clear, the method was known before Walker rose to fame. BB includes a three-page description of the method by Flt. Lt. Burton, writing in the mid-1940s, of captures of carp to 39lb (abroad) on floating crust.

Forceps are perfect for a difficult job like this.

Walker and his group – inevitably – took the technique and refined it into one of the central pillars of carp fishing. Walker also added that extra dimension of margin fishing, based on his observations that carp come into the windward shore to look for food scraps late at night. His memorable photograph of a carp, half out of the water, sucking crust from the bank, awakened a great many specialist anglers to new possibilities. Certainly, when I began carp fishing in the 1960s, the two methods every serious man used were either a large freelined bait or a surface-fished crust. Of my own first thirty carp, all but one came from the surface.

The 1960s and 1970s saw the crust boom continue. Bubble floats were used to give extra distance and the anchored crust was pioneered. Nottingham's Archie Braddock even caught twenty-pounders from the top in the winter. At the time, twenty years ago, this was considered an almost impossible break-through. Naturally, carp the length and breadth of the land began to wise up and crusts were coloured and flavoured and cast out further in response.

The real answers lay elsewhere. In the 1970s, *The Carp Film* was made by, among others, Roy Johnson. This featured the capture of a large fish off the surface on a piece of specially prepared cake. Specialized floating baits now took the method into its next common, more sophisticated stage. Developments over the past years have concentrated on different baits and refined presentations and just about every major carping brain has struggled with the problems at one time or another.

Chris Ball is probably the most experienced user of floating bait in this country and here he gives for us a brief run-down of his favourites.

'The sheer range of baits and their application in surface fishing for carp is massive, for, make no mistake, carp will investigate anything that floats. For years baits such as floating crust were the norm: I used to use the hard outside corner of a loaf for it lasted a lot longer on the hook. Also, you might be surprised to learn that the carp anglers of those days used to make their own bread loaves, ones that had hard crust all the way round!

You have no need to make any bait today as nearly all your needs will be catered for out of a packet. I'm talking about the large range of preshaped pet foods and animal food pellets which offer the floater angler a first-class bait. I'm not forgetting the high protein "floater" cake that has many forms, but the sheer convenience that the packeted foods offer, with virtually no preparation needed, appeals to nearly everybody. By far the most popular is Chum Mixer which comes in different-sized boxes – or do as I do and buy it in 10-kilo bulk bags. This works out at a very

reasonable 35p per pound. The cheapness of Chum is bound to appeal to younger anglers or those who want to saturate a water. For those of you who also like to play around with flavours, you will find that Chum takes on flavours and colours very well. Here are some ways to prepare Chum or any of the dog and cat food mixes.

1 Straight from the packet. The carp can handle the hard biscuits in their raw state. In fact, I believe this can be an advantage as the fish love to crunch and grind the granite-like pieces of food. Possibly this makes them more addicted to the biscuit and sometimes a feeding response can be produced that is quite frightening.

2 Straight out of the packet but oversprayed, using an atomizer of your chosen flavour. I use ten quick sprays out of the bottle into a bag containing one pound dry weight of mixers. This produces the lightest of coats which disperses quickly and can produce a devastating effect.

3 You can soak the mixers and introduce a flavour at the same time. An excellent method entails placing around one and a half pounds of dry mixers in a clear, airproof bag. Then introduce 150ml of water plus a flavour and if you like, a colour too. Shake the bag for three or four minutes so that every bait is covered. You will notice that the inside of the bag will appear to go dry. Now leave for an hour and there you have your own unique mixes to use. This method produces a soft but durable bait, one you can impale directly on to the hook.

4 Remember that there is a case to be made for the introduction of a sweetener to any floater. The fact that carp like sweet baits is well known, so bear this in mind as you prepare your floating baits.

Good luck, and remember there is nothing to beat taking a carp off the top.'

Ready-to-use floating baits.

A carp homes in on the area.

Chum Mixers are every bit as good for rudd as for carp, though rudd are not quite as inquisitive and need time to take them freely. Also, good conditions are even more important for rudd: a chop on the surface, rain, a cool breeze or even a lack of warm sunlight all make the species disinclined to feed in the surface layers. In addition, rudd are very wary of entering open water and spend most of the daylight hours holed up in areas they regard as sanctuary. Places to look for are the fringes of inaccessible weed and reed beds, around the far sides of islands, under remote beds of lilies and particularly in among the branches of fallen trees. In short, any area that sees little disturbance and few baits is worth investigation.

Very often the best way to approach these areas is by boat. It is vital to come up close to a rudd shoal with the greatest possible caution. Do not think of using an outboard, even an electric one, and make sure you row very slowly. Anchor as far away as possible and try to arrange to have the wind at your back. This is important because my first approach will always be with floating baits and, with the wind behind me, I can drift free offerings into the sanctuary area without spooking the shoal in any way.

Often it takes ten to fifteen minutes before the Chum begins to be taken and perhaps a hundred biscuits have gone over before the first one is sucked down.

I use a light 11–13 foot rod and 3 or 4lb line, well greased, straight through to a size 10 hook with a biscuit sitting on the shank. For casting weight, a small bubble float filled with the necessary amount of water cannot really be bettered. I aim to drop my own bait a few yards short of the taking area and let it make its own way on the breeze into the fish. I watch the bubble float and strike as it moves off or even occasionally study the bait through binoculars.

This method has worked well on those broads that still have large rudd in them. The old 'Crabtree' method was to anchor crust on a string and stone in the margins and wait until it was attacked by a passing shoal. For the life of me, I cannot see how this worked. I have tried it but the crusts are invariably consumed by the myriad water fowl that the broads are home to. Quite how it worked in the olden days I am not sure and I much prefer the Chum Mixer approach.

Presentation

Although this is a book about the bait and not presentation it is possibly justifiable to mention a little about the floater technique as this is not always fully understood. Obviously, if a floating bait can be fished hard against a reed, weed or lily bed then the problem of presentation is completely eased. Sadly, though, this is rarely possible in real fishing terms and usually you are forced to fish your floaters out in the open water.

Firstly, try to position yourself correctly according to the prevailing wind conditions. Ideally, you need to be on some type of promontory with a light-to-moderate wind behind you. If there is any breezy crosswind, it is almost bound to lead to poor bait presentation which is spotted by the fish a mile off. Very often a wind lane, the strip of calm water between waves, will prove to be a hot taking point, so look out for these as well.

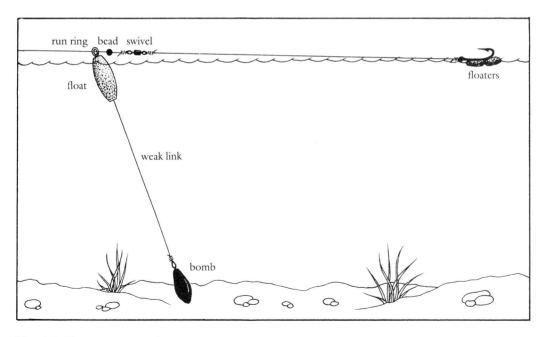

Fig. 4.1 Float paternoster rig.

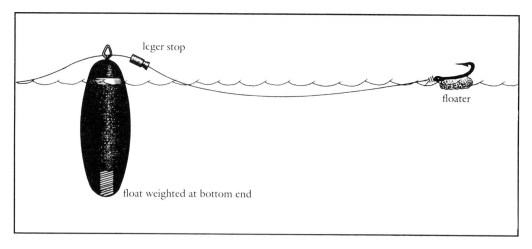

leger stop

floater

float weighted at bottom end

Fig. 4.2 Surface controller.

It is unproductive to spread pouchfuls of Mixers all over the water. It is far better to flick out half a dozen close into your bank and let them drift out over the lake for a few yards before repeating the process. After a while you will have established a line of them drifting tightly out over the water. Carp mostly work upwind and will take the first few baits very gently indeed so it is worth watching them through binoculars. As excitement grows, the carp will rise higher in the water and perhaps show their backs through the ripples. Activity is on the increase and now it is time to cast your own bait out. I say cast, but it is best dropped in close with the other baits to let the wind drift it out naturally (Fig. 4.1). You are actually trotting your bait out to the carp rather than casting it. Obviously, a long rod and greased line are essential for this work.

Wherever possible, watch the Chum Mixer biscuit, or whatever, rather than your controller float (Fig. 4.2). Binoculars are more than useful for this. The carp will very often mouth your biscuit gently and reject it without even moving the float. A take can easily be missed without any strike being made unless the mixer biscuit is watched with eagle eyes.

Watch the way that carp take the biscuits very closely. I have already said they start carefully and begin to crescendo. It is at the start of the rise in interest that you need to drift your own biscuit out. Hopefully, your bait will arrive in the taking area when the carp are at their most frenetic. This is when they will take a hook-bait with the least possible suspicion and your chances are at their highest. If you cast too soon you stand the chance of a wary fish ignoring the bait. If you cast too late, the first keenness of appetite is over and once again they will view floating baits with a certain amount of wariness and even disdain. On today's hard-fished waters, your biscuit also has to be presented properly. Think very carefully about whether the hook should be in the bait or whether the bait should be hair-rigged in some fashion. You might want to use the various ways of suspending the line from the water close into the bait. There might be a case for using a lighter than normal hook length or even Drennan Double Strength. All in all, floater fishing for carp, rudd or any species calls for a great deal of thought, observation and flexibility of approach.

Opening the magic can of sweetcorn.

PARTICLES

That great carp angler Lee Jackson is a great believer in particle baits as an alternative to boilies on some of the harder waters. Here he briefly explains the basics of his approach:

'Firstly, what are particles? Carp feed naturally on small food items. They are eaten in preference to everything else because they are usually in greater abundance, hence the name particles. With particles, the angler is aiming to imitate this natural food by providing a chosen food source that can be ground-baited in large quantities. This sort of presentation is nigh on impossible with boilies because they cannot be made in the quantities that would be required. Even if they could, the cost would certainly be immense.

Particles are generally small, and therefore their success is due to their numbers; imagine a pound of boilies in comparison to a pound of sweetcorn. Obviously, the sweetcorn provides many more individual food items and consequently there is a lot more attraction. The fish will become less cautious the more they feed on it.

The list of particle-type baits is endless as many varieties have been tried with varying degrees of success from water to water. The most common types in use are the various beans, seeds and nuts. Here are a few of them:

My favourites: Black-eyed beans, chick peas, dun peas, hazelnuts, maple peas, maize, groats, peanuts (*see* Figs 4.3 and 4.4), hempseed, sweetcorn, mini maple peas, tiger nuts, Canadian yellow peas, popping corn.

Chick peas and trout pellets – excellent particles.

Others: Butter beans, Brazil nuts, broad beans, cashew nuts, dari seeds, gunga peas, haricot beans, rape seeds, kidney beans, soya beans, buckwheat, tares, almonds.
Alternatives: Dolly mixtures, prawns, sultanas, jelly babies.

Many angling clubs impose bans on particle-type baits nowadays, most of them, in my opinion, being unjustified.

In a few isolated cases fish have died due to eating particle-type baits which have not been properly prepared by the angler using them. It is vitally important to take the utmost care when preparing particles. All nuts, beans, peas and seeds – unless they have come out of tins – should be soaked in water for at least twenty-four hours before they are used or, in the case of those that need it, placed in boiling water.

The reason for this soaking is because most nuts, beans and peas will absorb water and then swell up. Obviously, a fish with a gut full of unswollen beans will have a bit of a digestion problem, which in some cases could prove fatal. So the right preparation must be undertaken.

Most particle baits can be obtained fairly cheaply from health food shops or Continental-type food stores, although for bulk deals you are better off going to a particle bait specialist. These include Kent Particles of Orpington and Hinders of Swindon. It's worth asking their advice about the preparation of baits.

You can actually experiment with your particle baits by adding various flavours and attractors to them. This should be carried out as soon as the baits have been soaked. If boiling is required, the same water should be used. In the past, I have found success with peanuts dyed red and then flavoured with either maple cream, liquorice or Rod Hutchinson's Regular Sense Appeal, and with chick peas flavoured with either onion or banana. Obviously, the combinations are endless. Try experimenting with your own particular favourite attractors.

Tiger nuts – carp love them.

The close-up of chick peas.

Chick peas sprouted – an excellent alternative.

Sprouted mong beans make the perfect particle bait.

Presentation with particles is basically the same as it is for boilies although with the smaller seeds such as hemp, hook-baits should be prepared at home with a few spares just in case.

With particles it is preferable to fish with short hook links of maybe only four to six inches because of the nature in which the fish feed on them. For example, the fish move around very little while gorging themselves on the free offerings. It is often the case that the hook-bait is taken beyond the throat teeth, in which case the hook link will be chomped off, hence the term 'bite-off'.

Groundbaiting is best done with a catapult rather than a throwing stick. For long-range baiting it is advisable to use some form of bait-dropper. This can be used on a spare rod and can also have the advantage of being a marker when casting out your hook-bait.

There are no rules determining how much groundbait to put out before commencing fishing. As a general rule, with the large particles such as tiger nuts I usually catapult six or seven pouchfuls and then top it up if any rod-bending action results. With smaller particles like hemp I usually start with quite a bit more, usually 2lb which is quite a few pouchfuls.

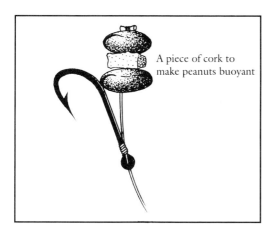

A piece of cork to make peanuts buoyant

Fig. 4.3 Buoyant peanuts.

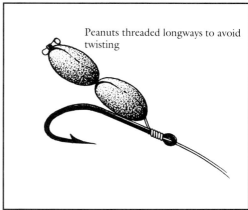

Peanuts threaded longways to avoid twisting

Fig. 4.4 Peanuts threaded longways.

Some anglers like to fish a boilie hook-bait over the top of a bed of particles. This can occasionally be successful. Personally I prefer to fish with particles on the hook as I'm sure the fish sometimes clear all the free offerings but leave the hook-bait. This is especially noticeable with small particles. They are much more likely to "hoover up" a particle-baited hook along with the loose offerings than they would a boilie that stands out.'

Hemp

Lee mentions using a large hook-bait over a bed of particles for carp and, of course, this approach is common to all species. Barbel in particular respond to a bait over a bed of hemp. The hook-bait itself can be of many different types; the important thing is that the barbel are hoovering up the hemp and do not consider the hook-bait too closely. Lobworms, maggots, special pastes, luncheon meat and even sweetcorn all work well over a bed of hemp. Steve Harper has his own tip about how to lay this bed:

'I'm very keen on catching more than one barbel in a session on my local River Wensum. Most anglers lay a bed of hemp as a round carpet which I think is wrong. I lay the hemp as

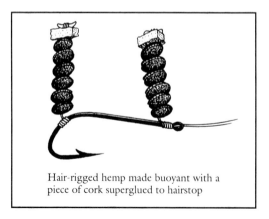

Hair-rigged hemp made buoyant with a piece of cork superglued to hairstop

Fig. 4.5 Hair-rigged buoyant hemp.

a long thin strip through the swim so that the barbel move along it in line. I then place my hook-bait at the top of the strip of hemp. I fish close to the rod tip which is pointing downstream, which is important, towards the head of the hemp strip. As a barbel works up the carpet it comes to my bait and I strike away from it towards the bank. The barbel, therefore, does not feel pressure coming from directly in front of it, but rather from the side. This makes the fish generally bolt straight away upstream.

Such an approach has two distinct advantages. Firstly, a barbel that moves upstream is a barbel landed. One that moves downstream, however, goes under branches, under trees and is impossible to pull out against the current. Secondly, by bolting upstream, the barbel leaves the swim and its shoal companions happily feeding. In this way, I can easily get a good number of fish from a swim before the shoal gets spooked and moves off. All this from just altering the shape of the hemp carpet!'

Hemp is perhaps the most universal of particle baits making them feed in an almost suicidal manner at times. Even the water that hemp is boiled in is useful. Ron Lees says:

'After boiling hempseed, most anglers will throw the water away. This can be put to excellent use in mixing groundbait. It must first be cooled and then a small amount of the hemp water should be poured into a groundbait bowl, adding cereal until the required consistency is obtained. Any large lumps can be removed by hand, or even sieved out. Keep these to try as hook-bait in paste form and you may be very pleasantly surprised. The result of all this will be a groundbait which contains hemp oil, tiny particles of the kernel of the seed and is an inexpensive way of producing your own additive.'

Particles splash around a lily bed.

Rice

We are talking repeatedly of particle beds, that is of carpets of tiny, attractive foods that draw fish into the swim and induce them to feed there. One of the best and least used of these attractive particles is rice, either white or brown grained. Rice is cheap, it is easily prepared and its grains are numerous, tiny and attractive to all species of fish. In fact, a pound of dry rice will produce a particle bed sufficient to keep bream, tench or carp working for hours. The grains simply get everywhere, even clinging to strands of weed, and keep fish hunting for them for a whole session.

It is essential that the rice is not overboiled: it simply needs to be softened, drained and rinsed immediately so the grains do not stick together but rather remain quite separate. At the cooking stage, the rice can be flavoured with a few drops of pineapple, maple or strawberry essence, for example, but the scent of the rice itself is generally quite sufficient.

Rice provides a perfect bed for nuts, casters, tares, corn or even a larger bait such as flake or lobworm. It is light, though, and is spread best at distance from a boat. From the bank, it can be glued by a light groundbait and catapulted long distances. Obviously immobile, the grains of rice do nothing to break up the balls in flight. I have tried rice on the hook, an almost impossible task, and certainly fruitless. It is rather like legering a blade of grass in a field for a cow!

The bulk freezing of hemp, wheat and other seeds which have been pre-cooked is possible, providing they are spread evenly and thinly on to trays and then frozen for twenty-four hours. After this they can be packed away into plastic bags and deep frozen normally. Prepared in this way, the grains will remain separate and will not settle into a solid block, which is by far the most wasteful way of freezing since the whole bulk must be defrosted regardless of the amount actually required for a fishing session.

Sweetcorn

Sweetcorn has over the last twenty or so years been such a massively successful bait that research has been made into who exactly first started using it. This is not easy. In his book *Tench*, Fred J. Taylor mentioned the use of maize, uncooked, in the United States. He said: 'There is no doubt, however, carp love the stuff and two grains on a number 6 hook will take them by day or night. I see no reason why it should not work over here too and I am quite sure tench would respond given the chance.'

By the early 1970s Jack Hilton and such close companions as Bill Quinlan were experimenting with small baits at Redmire. Their thinking was obvious: the carp in this marvellous water had been educated by anglers for twenty or more years and had become very wary of large baits. Obviously, they would not pick up many pieces of luncheon meat, potato or bread before being hooked and being made wary of that same bait in the future. However, with much smaller baits many more would be consumed until the trauma of being hooked occurred. The other bonus of small baits – soon to become known as particle baits – was that they closely resembled the tiny natural foodstuffs on which carp, tench and bream, for example, feed on for so much of the summer.

F. J. Taylor, one of the pioneers of sweetcorn in this country.

Accordingly, Jack Hilton and the Redmire crew began to look at smaller baits and soon they were having considerable success with maggots. Maggots, of course, pose their own problems. They are not an easy bait to keep without refrigeration in the summer through a long session and they are quite non-specific in the fish they attract. In January 1972 *The Angling Telegraph* ran an article by Ron Clay. Ron had been a big carping name in the 1950s and 1960s but had gone to live abroad, and he related his experiences of carp catching he had come across in South Africa: 'Most of the bigger carp were taken on grains of sweetcorn, about three on a number 4 hook.'

The most famous fish ever caught on sweetcorn; Chris Yates's 51lb record.

It was in June of that same year that sweet-corn first made its appearance at Redmire. The rumour has always been that it was Chris Yates who discovered the bait and used it there first. In all probability, Chris's inventive mind simply picked up on an idea that was already beginning to bubble.

All this, however, is academic. What really matters is that sweetcorn is in many ways the ultimate particle bait. Carp, tench, bream, barbel, roach, rudd ... all fish species with the exception of true predators seem to enjoy sweetcorn and this suggests there is some-thing in the bait that they positively appreci-ate. A can of corn also contains many grains and it is therefore quite possible that the fish is only hooked after consuming one or even two or three hundred mouthfuls. Corn, for this reason, has a comparatively long life as the fish do not immediately associate it with danger after being caught.

Corn is easily and comparatively cheaply obtainable. There is not a village shop or a supermarket in the land that does not offer cans of corn for sale. Fresh corn can be used, even off the cob if it is cooked and separated. However, canned corn is still the most popular form of the bait, possibly because of its extreme sweetness. In fact, hot weather only seems to increase canned corn's efficiency. The stickier and smellier the concoction becomes, the more fish seem to fall for it.

Obviously the species being sought dictates the number of pieces of corn used and the size of hook. Roach, for example, will take a small piece on a size 16 whereas a barbel or a carp will frequently be tempted by three or four grains on a size 4 or 6. It is very much up to the individual angler to vary the bait and the approach to the particular water and species being tackled. Talking of hooks, there are now gilt hooks on the market, supposedly perfect for sweetcorn use. I personally have found them no better than bronze.

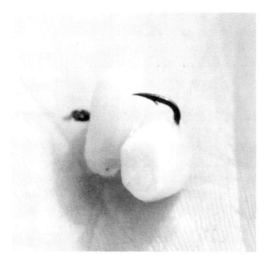

Double sweetcorn snugly fitting the hook.

The big question with corn is how much free bait to introduce into the water. Views vary. Rod Hutchinson for example, used to bombard a water with corn in an effort to switch every fish in front of him over to that foodstuff. On the other hand, Chris Yates used a more careful approach, just sprinkling a few grains here and there as he went around the lake. Both approaches are equally valid in certain situations and I personally have found heavy baiting with corn to be very effective for carp but not, however, for tench. One particularly massive prebaiting with corn for tench produced an absolute blank. The corn was bought in large caterers' tins and pounds were put in over the course of a week. The tench totally evacuated the area! Chub, seemingly, can eat corn day long. Barbel, too, adore the stuff in quite large quantities especially if used over a carpet of hemp.

Corn is infinitely flexible. For example, when fishing over a mud or soft weed bottom the bait should sink very slowly and not become buried. This is done by substituting a piece of yellow polystyrene for a grain of corn in a group of three or four particles. Also, where corn is beginning to be regarded with suspicion, it is a perfect bait to take colourings and flavourings. Red corn, in particular, I have found has given the bait extended life.

Loose corn can be catapulted a fair distance but ice cubes made up of sweetcorn and stored in a vacuum flask can be catapulted vast distances and still kept in a very tight area.

After twenty-odd hard years of usage, the initial impact of sweetcorn has obviously worn away. Most fish in club or day ticket waters have seen corn and probably been caught on it at some stage in their lives. The question is, therefore, whether corn still has a valuable future. Obviously it has. Maggots and bread, for example, still catch fish centuries after their introduction and corn is a bait that will be with us for as long as angling exists.

5 The Predators

LIVEBAITS

The question of livebaiting for pike, perch and zander is the hottest question in angling today. Already livebaiting has been banned in Ireland and in many club waters in England and Wales. The reasoning is easy to see: livebaits can spread disease and some escape and spark off populations in waters where they are totally undesirable. Furthermore, livebaits are often taken from waters that can ill afford them and stocks plummet startlingly quickly.

There also remains a moral issue. Hooking and casting a live fish to its probable death is not a pleasant business. I do livebait and I will continue to do so until the day it might become illegal but I'm not proud of myself for doing so. A memory lingers on: I'd used a rainbow trout for three hours and it was

Small fry rise before a marauding predator.

tired and half dead when it was taken by a twenty-pound pike. I retrieved the bait from the jaws and used it as a deadbait. Two hours later I prepared to cast it yet again and, as it swung in front of me I saw its eye move quite deliberately. I checked the fish and it quivered. After five hours on the hooks, several casts and a severe mauling, life still lingered on. I felt physically sick for it.

The fact remains that there are waters that only respond to livebaits. Clear trout waters are a case in point where the ratio between live and deadbait successes can be twenty or more to one. Without livebaits on waters such as these, fishing is pretty much a waste of time. Also, it has to be said that in the wild most fish species are predatorial at one time or another. This is the law of nature and anglers or legislation will not change it at all. Indeed, the livebaiting angler is seen by many simply as a man in tune with nature's often cruel workings.

Perhaps the best thing is to be careful about how livebaits are procured and we must make sure that this is done in the future in a sensible manner. For generations, each angler has snatched his baits from the environment in any way that has presented itself, often with dire side effects. There has been a lot of disease spread and waters have been depopulated. The rational way to obtain livebaits is to buy them from fish farms where they can be bred, disease free, for this very purpose. In this way natural populations would be freed and disease be contained. The pike angler would be forced to pay for his bait but then, catching them is a costly business in terms of time, hook-bait and travelling. Simple purchase would be quick, clean and environmentally preferable. Whatever way the livebait is procured, it is precious and it must be kept as safely as possible and certainly not be allowed to die wastefully.

Back in 1971, in *Fishing for Big Pike*, Rickards and Webb illustrated the keeping of livebaits either in a polythene bait container with holes punched in it placed in a garden pond or in an aerated horse trough in the garage. I personally have kept fish alive throughout the winter in old baths and, in particular, the water tanks that are used in lofts. All of these hold well over thirty gallons of water and are able to accommodate thirty to fifty small fish quite satisfactorily. Transportation of livebaits to the water is another important issue which I will leave to John Watson who for years took baits successfully around the country before this was made illegal. This piece still has relevance, however, for those moving baits along the same water course or around very large stillwaters.

Transporting Livebait

'Bait fish can be extremely difficult to catch during the winter months and, therefore, being able to take them with you is obviously a great advantage. There is no point in going for a weekend's fishing and spending half the time trying to catch baits.

The transportation of live fish (if the Water Authority permits it) for use either as livebaits or as freshly killed deadbaits is a problem which confronts a lot of pikemen. The use of a battery-operated air pump has, over the last few years, made things a bit easier, but the number of baits that can be transported from home to the water and kept in peak condition

during a long journey is limited due to the amount of air the popular models are capable of pumping through. It's no use starting a journey with a bucket full of prime baits only to arrive at the destination to find that half of them have "croaked" *en route*. The fact that some of the baits are going to spend the next day or so in captivity before their turn arrives to become "pike fodder" also necessitates the need for them to be in top condition.

I do most of my piking away from home, spending the winter months in Licensing or on the Fens and, as was the case last year, the closed season on Loch Lomond. Both journeys involve a drive of up to five hours, and five hours' sloshing about in a bucket in the back of my van can certainly take it out of even the best bait-fish!

Some of my first expeditions to the Fens saw me arriving with a bucketful of dead and semi-dead fish. Roach and dace seemed to be the worst travellers and sometimes out of two or three dozen in a bucket, only half of them would survive the journey. Lack of oxygen was the problem.

The best pump available, though not really powerful enough for my requirements, retailed at about £10; to buy a couple of these, plus a supply of batteries would not leave much change from £25. I therefore sought an alternative which, when it turned up, came in the form of an electrically operated S.u. petrol pump, e.g. the type used in a Mini or 1100.

These pumps can be easily obtained from a scrapyard for a few bob – mine cost 50p. Fitting and wiring up was no problem even for me and was done as follows. First of all, decide on the most convenient place to put it; mine is lodged between a bulkhead and the side of my van, just behind the driver's seat. It can either be bolted to the floor or jammed into some convenient corner. Ensure, however, that it is stable and that the intake hole is not

Chris Turnbull holds a good river-caught pike.

blocked. If it does get blocked or covered in any way the pump will start to smoke.

I've fitted a small brass connector into the "blow" hole to which I've affixed a length of plastic tubing, the type readily obtained from any aquarist's shop. A "T" piece is then fixed to the other end, thus allowing for two airlines to be used at once if required.

Wiring up is straightforward. Mine is connected, via an on/off switch on the dashboard, to the battery and is earthed by a small hole in the bodywork in a convenient spot. Connection is by a short length of wire from the base of the pump to this hole by means of a self-tapping screw.

If you're lucky and pick up a pump in good condition, it can last you for years: the one I've got in my van now is in its fourth year. The only

apparent fault that's likely to occur is for the contacts to burn out. If they do go, it's easier to fit a fresh pump than to try to fit new contacts.

The amount of air the pump pushes through has to be seen to be believed. I use a couple of 6in-long airstones and the air really belts through. It can also be used to blow up inflatable dinghies, air beds and the like, so the next time you pass a scrapyard or see a battered Mini lying in some ditch, treat yourself and you will probably catch more pike as a result.

To keep livebaits fresh while fishing overnight on a two- or three-day trip, place a piece of net curtain over the bucket, in place of the lid, and secure with elastic. Tie a length of rope to the handle, and the other end to a rod rest, and the bucket can then be lowered safely to some depth.'

Martyn Page's Livebait Tips

Martyn believes that half the battle of live-baiting is to get the fish to the water in a healthy, robust state. A tatty bait, or one that is about to expire at any moment, is of little use. He is also adamant that it is important to match the bait with the water and season. For example, in warm water crucians cannot be beaten but they are not nearly as good in cold water when they virtually go to sleep and hardly work at all.

For Martyn, dace are probably the best of all if there is reasonable oxygen content in the water. A hot, still broad in high summer is therefore not dace livebaiting water. Dace are also of a perfect swallowing shape! Cynical as this sounds, they do slide down the pike throat second to none! Small chub – if they are obtainable – are almost as good.

In shallow water, Martyn likes rudd better than anything else as they work very quickly to the top and present an enticing sight to the pike beneath. However, if fished deep they will continue to try to get to the top and tangle any rig known. In deeper water, therefore, roach are a much better bet.

Trout are an expensive bait and frequently too boisterous for a lazy pike. However, Martyn feels they are a good 'wind-up' bait. By that he means that they will excite an otherwise lethargic pike into an attack on a smaller bait placed close beside.

If Martyn were limited to the use of just one bait, he would probably choose those small hybrid carp that exist in many farm

This is the way they treat pike in Scotland!

ponds. It is hard to decipher whether they are commons or crucians, or even small mirrors. They're tough and will work all day if the pike allow!

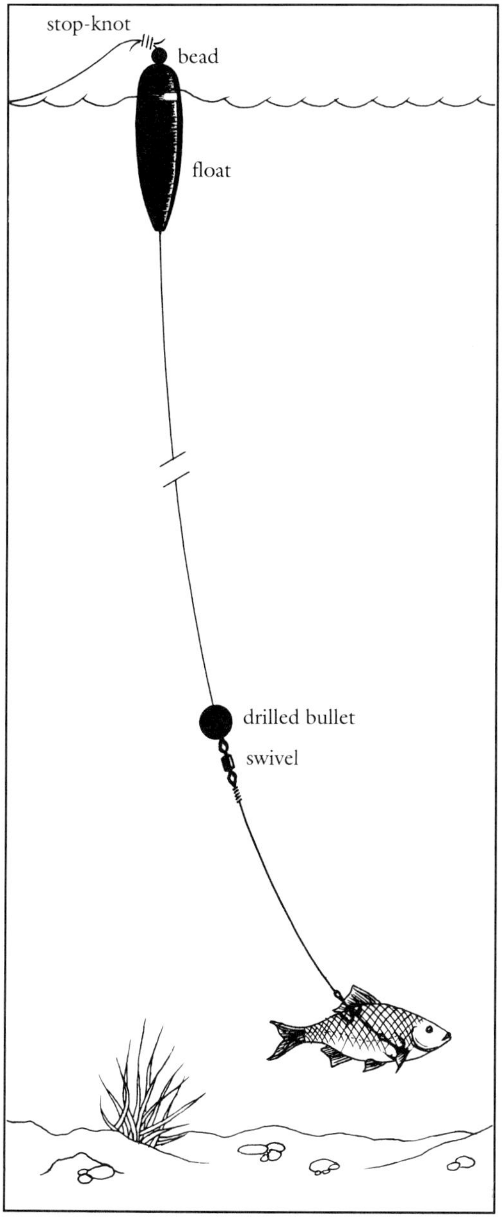

For trailing on the rivers, Martyn believes the crucian are brilliant. Their erratic, jabbing swimming motion excites the pikes' curiosity. Furthermore, their tight swimming action means that they are rarely missed by the attacking pike and most takes are converted into a fish to the boat.

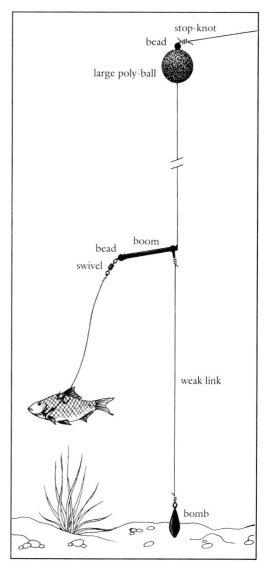

Fig. 5.1 Roving livebait rig.

Fig. 5.2 Sunken float paternoster rig.

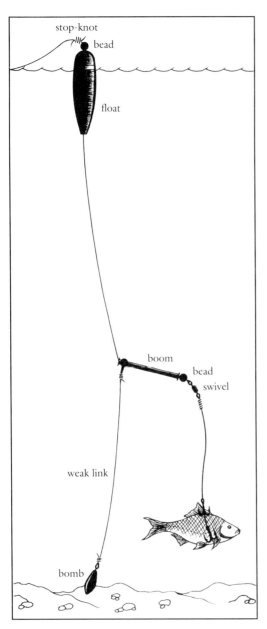

Fig. 5.3 Standard livebait rig.

PLUGS, SPOONS AND SPINNERS

Lure fishing has been the growth area in angling over the past year and the boom looks set to continue. Big names such as Gord Burton, Barry Rickards, Chris Liebbrandt and Charlie Bettell have done a wonderful job in helping the average angler towards some exhilarating sport. Furthermore, as more and more livebait bans are imposed, lure fishing will assume ever greater significance, especially in clear waters where deadbaits rarely work.

Choosing the right lure for the job can be the most daunting task to the newcomer who looks at the vast array available. Fortunately, soon to be published by the Crowood Press is a guide to several hundred lures, compiled by Chris and Sue Harris. Chris and Sue took a monumental gamble and left executive jobs to found their mail-order lure business. Orders have flooded in and they give a quick, efficient, friendly service. Do not hesitate to ring them on 0692 581208, presuming this chapter does not satisfy your every need! Hopefully it will go some way towards it, thanks to the expert start given by Chris Liebbrandt:

'In keeping with most introductions to lure angling, a few words should be said about the types of rod to use. Any lightish carp rod (1½–2lb tc) of 10–12 feet will do. The reason for the (so-called) soft rods is the penchant that pike have for attacking lures when only feet from the rod tip. This means that you will need a rod that will bend and these softer rods are ideal.

I never use line of less than 12lb test, more usually 15–17lb. The great advances in line technology mean that these tests are not as outrageous as they first appear. Most of the new co-polymer lines offer lower diameters and this is really useful when heavier lines on fixed-spool reels are a bit playful.

Martin Gay and Barry Rickards, pioneers in the artificial lure scene.

Now we have a carp rod and reel loaded with line, what lure should we choose? Some lure fanatics, and I am one of them, have ridiculous amounts of baits; indeed, I get myself confused. A little thought on the subject can give you a lot of pointers and a quick look at the origins of lures will help. Over 85 per cent of them come from America, with the other 15 per cent being mainly Scandinavian in origin.

Most of the lures that are available have been designed for large and smallmouth bass, a sort of American super perch with psychopathic tendencies towards food items! A lunker smallmouth will be 6lb and a double-figure largemouth is a very big fish, the record smallmouth being 11lb 2oz and largemouth 22lb 4oz. They are significantly smaller than pike and therefore prey on smaller food items and this is reflected in the size of the baits. A lot of the Scandinavian baits are designed with pike in mind and this is borne out by the generally larger lures.

Consideration should be given to the depth of water that you are going to fish and the nature of the vegetation that is going to afford shelter to the pike.

There are various lure types: surface, shallow, medium and deep divers, sinkers and neutral density lures. There are also spinners, spoons and spinnerbaits, all of which sink but can be worked in all layers of the water.

Surface

Surface lures are perhaps the expert's domain. They can be very difficult to use, as all too often the retrieve speeds are critical to the lure's action. Try the Heddon Torpedo and Dying Flutter which have the assistance of small propellers that make the water gurgle and fizz. Use in short bursts; the secret of success is the use of erratic retrieve patterns. Surface baits that have large tips or paddles walk or crawl over the surface of the water. The Heddon Crazy Crawler, Arbogast Jitterbug

A morning's trolling is about to begin.

and Luhr Jensen Dalton Twist are all good choices. My all-time favourite surface bait is, however, the Heddon Meadow Mouse; worked slowly around reed beds and lily pads it's a killer.

The next category, the floater/diver, make up the vast majority of lures available to the UK enthusiast, these can be shallow, medium or deep divers. Most plugbaits have a range of tip design so that the basic body shape can be fished at depths of 1–20 feet. Regardless of the diving vanes employed, there are certain basic body shapes that are familiar to most of us. There are subtle changes being made which refine the action of these lures, the overall shapes remaining fairly standard.

The most recognizable shape is that of the Minnow, made famous by the classic wood

Rapala Minnow. Every lure angler I know possesses at least one of these if not more and most casual anglers will have a copy of it in their box. Another favourite straight bait is the Creek Chub Pikie Minnow, which has a "thin" action, and the most recent improvement to the Minnow range has been an ultra-modern bait called the Rebel Black Star which with carbon fibre and light chambers is enough to make a traditionalist wood lure man blanch. I have a preference for wood baits and the best of the lot, Bagler's, are now available in this country, the Bank O Lure being their representative.

A new shape, but very popular, is the "alphabet" lure. Nearly every angler will have one of these, the most well known being the Shakespeare Big S. There are also Big Os, Big

Ns, Fat As, Wee Rs, Killer Bs and Big Ds (the last one is a peanut, just checking you're awake!). All these crank baits (so called because you cast them out and crank them in) have remained relatively unchanged since their introduction over twenty years ago. Use them in an erratic fashion, plenty of short sweeps of the rod tip away, trying to make sure you allow the bait lots of opportunity to float up to the surface. I get a lot of takes when the lure is doing this.

The last in the floater/diver section is the banana-shaped lure which relies on its body shape to plane it down and make it wobble. Kwikfish, Flatfish and Lazy Ike's were all designed to be used with an uptrace lead. This calms down the rather manic action and produces a totally different action, particularly when the lead is allowed to sink. The lure sways with a very gentle action – try it and see its effect.

Colours

Colours are always an interesting conversation point but I tend to favour very lifelike colours such as perchscale, shad and crawfish for big lures where the baits are retrieved at slower rate. On smaller baits, the more caricature or cartoon types of bait finish can be used: Pire Tiger, chrome and blue, redhead and finally black. Any chartreuse, big eyes and red throats are also helpful.

Sinking Lures

Sinking lures are now becoming more available. I am speaking here of specialist vibratory lures and not sinking versions of floaters. The Cotton Cordell Ratt'l Spot Minnow is now a firm favourite since its introduction into this country by T. G. Lures. This is a long thin version of the "Spot"-type lures. They sink

Who can doubt the efficiency of a plug!

quickly, cast like bullets and have fast vibratory actions. The retrieve method is one of counting them down to the required depth and then using them in a fast sink and draw. You may not feel much of an action, but they are working overtime.

One last thing about any type of lure angling: try to believe that the bait that you are using is alive. It's not a piece of wood, or plastic, but actually an injured fish, frog, mouse or duckling. Using this psychology and retrieving as slowly as possible, you will be surprised at how efficient your angling can be. It is also really good fun.'

Chris himself goes on to say that 'spinners, spoons and spinner bait are the other side of the lure angling coin and these are quite a different prospect to the plugbait side of things.' Charlie Bettell now takes up the discussion with his own guide to spinners and spoons.

A Guide to Spinners and Spoons

'One of the main reasons why spinners are neglected by novice and pro alike is the wide array of lovely-coloured plugs, spoons and spinner baits now available. I personally have favoured spoons and plugs at their expense over the last few years. Certain types of lure seem to possess mystical powers that make you keep on using them! The harder you try to break the habit, the more you're drawn to them, making some other lures redundant at a very young age. That seems to have been the case with me and spinners over the last few years, although I've been using spinner/wobbling baits to exhaustion.

Are there specific times or conditions to use spinners and spoons? In my mind there isn't a good time as such, but statistically speaking the right conditions are when the water is clearish and the sky bright. Catch results will suffer using spinners and spoons

This big trout fell to a deeply fished plug.

during low light and murky water conditions, compared with, say, that of a good vibratory plug, which can be retrieved much more slowly. Another type of condition to watch out for is jumping prey fish, which usually means that pike are on their tails.

I said "work a plug around the outside of a shoal of prey fish" and I still maintain that. With a spinner/spoon, though, I would recommend that you work it through the middle of the shoal. On sunny days, you'll often see roach, rudd and so on, follow your spinner/spoon all the way to the bank, which, in turn can create a hot spot very close in as the pike follow the prey. Can anybody tell me why fish that aren't classed as predators do that?

To get good catch results on the day, you must follow your results of old! What I mean by that is: you must remember what lure has produced fish for you in the past when fishing similar conditions. When you have a good day with a specific lure *make notes*: what are the water/weather conditions (i.e. clear, murky, warm, cold)? Are prey fish present? What lure are you using? Make a note of your lure's visual aspects with regard to water conditions and so on. Making notes and comparing them is the only way to come up with statistics that will help you in the future.

When I first started lure fishing, I used many types of spinner and spoon with which I had fairly good results considering the waters I was fishing. Most of my old spinners/spoons are now resting in retirement snags! I think I might have just put my finger on the main reason why spinners and spoons aren't used as much as plugs and spinnerbaits nowadays: snagging. Spinners and spoons are definitely more prone to snagging than plugs and spinnerbaits. There are ways around the problem, though. A controller float will almost eliminate the loss of a lure. You may catch less poundage using a controller float, but you'll save pounds.

The most productive season to use spinners and spoons is when we have a flux of fish in our rivers, lakes and pits. 1991–92 was a bumper fry season throughout the country. In the first four weeks of the 1991–92 season I caught sixty pike on a silver spoon. Gord Burton also had a great year using a copper spoon. Because there were so many prey fish available to the pike, top-water plug fishing was hard going, although I still managed a 25-pounder on a buzz stick. I've found, over the years, that if there's a flux of prey fish in a water, pike won't bother too much with top-water plugs, but when there's a shortage, the reverse can be expected.

I personally, don't keep good records of my catches throughout the season, but I known a man who does! I thought it would be nice for a change to show somebody else's

A big spoon accounted for this Irish monster.

catch rate in my article. John Worzencraft started lure fishing again last year after a long lay-off of twenty years and I must say now, for a person who hasn't fished for so many years, you'll find his statistics quite unbelievable. From September 1991 to March 1992 he caught 144 predators on spinners and 98 on plugs – 27 weeks, 242 pike.

A few snippets from John's statistics:

1 Largest pike: 19lb 13oz on a Mepps Comet Decoree red on gold.
2 Largest zander: 5lb on a Mepps Black Fury.
3 Largest perch: 2lb on a Mepps Comet No. 5 red on silver.
4 Most successful spinner: Mepps Comet Decoree.
5 Most successful plug: Big S type.
6 Most successful home-made plug: Hybrid plug spinner!
7 Rod: Silstar fly rod with butt extension. Different.
8 Number of weeks fished: 27.
9 Trips: 24.
10 Doubles: 27.
11 Fish under ten pounds: 215.
12 Total catch of predators: 242.

I must point out that John only used lures throughout the 1991–92 season. The waters John fished obviously played a major part in his high catch rate; unfortunately for you though, I'm sworn to secrecy. Good luck next season, John.

If you're just starting lure fishing, I would definitely start off with cheap lures. There's no quicker way of being put off lure fishing than by losing an expensive lure on its first cast. In my view, in the hands of a raw novice a £1.50–£3.00 spinner, spoon or plug can be just as effective as a dearer lure.

Expensive plugs usually need to be worked correctly in the right area and depth of water if good results are to be achieved. A raw novice does lack experience, so in my view, he should learn to walk before he tries to run. Spinners and spoons don't need experienced hands to get good results. So, if you have children or friends (raw novices) who you would like to get started, set them up with a top-water plug during the summer months, or a cheap spinner/spoon or diving plug in the summer or winter months, with a small controller float that will support the lure's weight.

There are three main types of spinner available (excluding spinnerbaits and buzzers) today. I'll go through them in order to help you appreciate their differences. Any of the following types of spinner can have a mixed blade combination.

1 Standard spinner with 1, 2 or 3 blades. The blades revolve around a weighted or unweighted wire shaft by means of a clevis.
2 Weight forward spinner has a weight forward of its spinning blade. It usually has only one blade mounted on it, but I have seen some with two.
3 Keel weighted spinner has the weight on its shaft weighted more on one side than the other. The additional weight helps to eliminate line twist on retrieve. Again, like the standard-type spinner, one, two or even three blades are common.

Blade rotation angles: Willow leaf and Lusox, 25 degrees; Anglia Long, 30 degrees; Indiana and French, 40 degrees; Comet and Black Fury, 45 degrees; Colorado, 50 degrees; Anglia, 60 degrees.

There's more:

Adjustable scissor blade: a blade with which the degree of rotation can be varied as can the size of the blade!

Buzz/counter turning blade: a type of spinning blade that is mounted directly on the wire shaft via two holes. Its angle of rotation is 180–360°.

Sonic blade: a blade that is mounted on the wire shaft via a single hole in the blade (no clevis required). The sonic blade is of a concave/convex shape.

Fluted blade: a distorted blade that creates extra reflection from it.

The broader the blade, the greater the angle of its rotation and the greater the resistance it will offer on retrieve. The larger the blade in a particular style, the more resistance it creates.

A spinner with a blade rotation of about 25–40 degrees is best when fishing fast flowing water. For slow-flowing or still waters, most types of blade are acceptable and, for shallow water, a Colorado-type spinner would be far better for slow retrieving work due to the blade's resistance. A spinner that has a high resistance to the angler will stay high in the water if retrieved straight away or just after contact with the water. A slow speed of retrieve can be rewarding when fishing shallow or slow-moving waters.

When fishing clear deep waters, I like to use big willow-leaf-type spinners because a

A close-up of Gord Burton's anti-kink vane.

willow-leaf blade has a lesser angle of rotation (about 25–30 degrees depending on blade width) and you get the maximum amount of flash from it.

As I've said, some spinners have one, two or even three blades mounted on the wire shaft. The extra blades help to up their flash, colour and vibration output. A skirt is another great asset to a spinner's visual aspect, although very few spinners seem to come skirted nowadays.

Spoons can be summed up very easily in my view. Use a heavyish-type (standard)

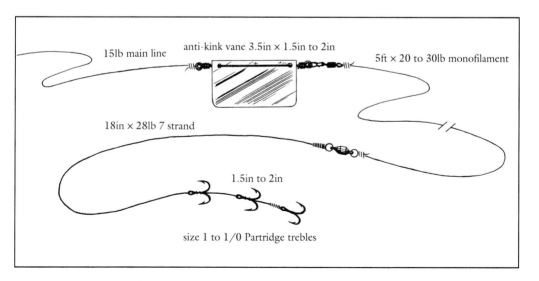

Fig. 5.4 Gord Burton's anti-kink vane rig.

spoon to get down deep in a hurry. I personally, don't use spoons over 2oz in weight. If a good action/vibration is required from a spoon at depth, use a lightweight (trolling) spoon. You'll have to wait about 30 seconds (in 30 feet of water) for a lightweight spoon to touch bottom before retrieving it, though.

When spoon fishing in shallow water, lightweight trolling spoons are a must.

As for colour of spoon, in clear water I personally like to use silver, gold or copper coloured, but other colours can be just as effective.

When fishing coloured water, I choose a spoon that can be seen at the greatest depth. When the water is very coloured I'll only use plugs.'

DEADBAITS

The use of deadbaits is not a twentieth-century development and was recommended as far back as the seventeenth century. However, deadbaits have certainly fallen out of favour for scores of years, though F. J. Taylor did a lot to revive interest in their use during the 1950s. Fred, apparently, was as amazed as anyone when the line to a dead roach began to move away to a taking pike! At the same period, other anglers totally ignorant of Fred's work, were moving towards the use of deads again. In Norfolk, notably, Bill Giles and Reg Sandys were starting to find that in certain conditions a deadbait could actually outfish a live one. A whole piking approach was being reborn and, today, captures of pike are probably equally divided between dead-baits and livebaits and artificial lures, an altogether healthy arrangement.

There is a never-ending list of types of fish that can be used to catch pike and, as more and more exotics are appearing in the fish shops each year, this list will be extended. There are, however, old favourites:

Roach, Dace and Chub

These are the old standards and are tough and universally popular baits. In today's pressured times, however, supplies of all these species should be collected with care. Most acceptably, they might be the casualties left over after a match or after some unfortunate pollution and fish kill. Another good time to collect supplies is after spawning or in the summer when oxygen levels are low and many small fish perish. They can be collected during these times and frozen until needed.

Small Pike

These can be anything from six inches in length to 2lb in weight, though the hooking of the latter is a nightmare. Obtaining such baits is not easy and there are pike anglers who see something criminal in using a dead *Esox* where they do not in using a dead roach. Big pike do, however, in the wild eat a great many of their own young and a more natural bait is hard to imagine. A possible source of unwanted dead 'pikelets' is the put-and-take trout fishery where pike are totally unwanted,

A well-stocked freezer is a boon to the pike angler in winter.

unpaying guests. Any small ones caught are killed at once and might just as well be frozen for you on request.

Rainbow Trout

This is an excellent deadbait easily obtainable from any fishmonger with little or no harm done to the environment apart from round the fish farm itself! Trout have the advantage of giving off a good deal of oil and flavour into the water. They are also a tough-skinned bait that withstand long casting.

Herrings and Mackerel

Once again, these are environmentally friendly, easily obtainable and give out excellent odours. By the 1980s a lot of pike had seen them used on a great many waters and their success was being reduced accordingly. However, they are always worth a try on large, heavily covered waters.

Sprats

These are consistently successful but often attract smaller pike. This is not a rule, however, and occasional monsters have fallen for the bait.

Smelts

These are the success story of the 1980s. They represent possibly the most successful of a new wave of baits that caught a great many very large fish. Smelts do tend to vary a good deal in both size and quality. Where possible select the biggest and the freshest.

Sardines

An excellent oily bait, though sometimes their softness makes line casting a problem.

Exotics

Any small fish that comes from anywhere in the world and ends up on the fishmonger's slab is well worth experimenting with. Indeed, the more unusual the bait the less likelihood there is of the pike being wary of it. The bait just cannot be too bizarre: a friend of mine in 1980 found his collection of goldfish dead one morning. These were frozen and used later on the River Thurne and caught several large fish that were untouched on more normal baits.

Sprats are best stored in packets of six, eight or ten, or whatever you consider sufficient for a day's fishing. Herrings are best in packets of three or four. Mackerel are better frozen separately and kept as straight as possible. If you suspect that long casting is going to be required, cut the fins and tails from the bait to keep the flight straighter through the air. Freshwater fish, especially roach and small bream, should be washed carefully and deslimed before being dried, graded and packed in the same way as sea fish. It also pays at this stage to reject any damaged fish. A cut fish becomes very soft when it defrosts and firm baits stand up to the whole process much better.

Moving Deadbaits

A deadbait does not need to be fished static to produce good results. In fact, moving a deadbait is often the most effective way of triggering off a take. A deadbait can be spun just like an artificial lure but, more importantly, it can be moved in a slow enticing fashion. Peter Hancock caught his one-time record pike from Horsey Mere by using a very slow retrieve. He inched the bait along the bottom, moving it every couple of minutes or so, and the giant took. Despite this success and

A mid twenty-pounder that fell to a trout livebait.

many others before and since, it is more normal to leave baits static and festering on the bottom.

Robin Revell many years ago did a great deal of work with moving deadbaits and here he tells of his conclusions.

'Just how do you make a deadbait move? The simplest way is probably to use a float. This not only provides something to look at and liven up a day's fishing, it also enables you to cover a lot of water around your chosen patch. Admittedly, you're at the twin mercies of wind and current but the bait is roving around and doing something different from its partner which is quietly decomposing on the bottom.

A float can also provide a handy way of fishing a sink-and-draw method. A quick glance at Fig. 5.5 will show you what I'm getting at. If you're fishing at a short distance, either from the bank or from a bait, and there are a few weed beds that warrant exploring, then judicious use of a sliding float can pay

There are times when it pays to take it easy.

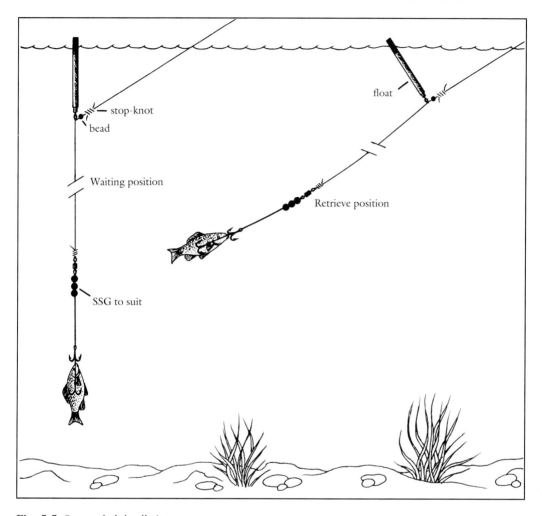

Fig. 5.5 Suspended deadbait.

real dividends. You may have to grease the line to make the ploy work properly, but it works and it's a technique that I employ regularly on those rare occasions ,when I'm afloat. It's simplicity itself. Raising the rod tip raises the bait, which can then be left to drop naturally. I've caught several fish on the drop using the method and you can use it just about anywhere. For instance, it's caught me fish from under the rod tip on my local gravel pits.

A naturally sinking bait can be quite deadly – but so, too, can a buoyant one. Sometimes the bait hasn't ruptured its swim-bladder and floats like a cork. This can be infuriating when the bait is frozen and you're doing your darndest to make the wretched thing sink – but it can work for you as well as against you. A buoyant bait can be quite deadly when legered. On a running line it will float up off the bottom and you can then pull it back down again to your heart's content. Force-feeding the deadbait with expanded polystyrene is probably the best way to give buoyancy – you can then predetermine the bait's buoyancy in a plastic bucket. A slightly buoyant bait can be made to flutter most enticingly just off the bottom. It's a method that zander seem to find attractive and it is a very good way of avoiding eels. More to the point, it also catches pike. In a snag-free water, you can employ this method to fish a slow-motion sink-and-draw technique. Fig. 5.6 illustrates what I mean. This method doesn't really have a lot to offer over a standard sink-and-draw technique, but I found it quite deadly in the shallows of Loch Lomond when trying to avoid the ravages of eels.

Fig 5.7 shows what I consider the best way to make a deadbait move. By fishing a buoyant bait just off the bottom, you can fish hard against a fish-holding structure. Whether the fish feature is a weed bed, sunken tree or a hopeful-looking gravel bar is immaterial. You cast judiciously in the chosen spot and tweak the bait about hopefully near where there

should be predatory pikey eyes. It is far superior to livebait as far as I'm concerned as the agonized bait is feigned by low-down cunning.

I hope I'm putting across the idea that moving the bait is fun. All too often a deadbaiting session takes on the mantle of an endurance event. I am absolutely positive that anyone who uses electronic bait-indicators must be thoroughly bored with his fishing. After dark perhaps – but in broad daylight? Perhaps it's the fault of those massed ranks of rods again. You can't watch them all at the same time, after all.'

The increased used of deadbaits has led to some sort of a revolution. Jim Hickey explains how today's tackle shops offer a large and varied range of coarse and sea baits, blast frozen and, more often than not, vacuum packed for freshness.

'Freshness of bait is of paramount importance. Should bait be old or of poor quality, the flesh will become soft and useless,

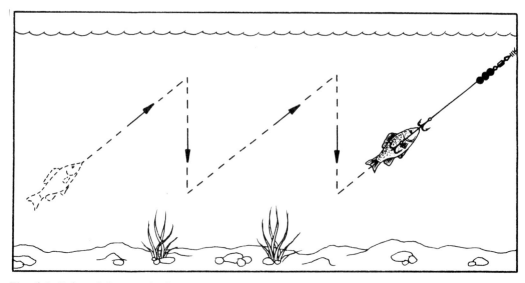

Fig. 5.6 Sink-and-draw method.

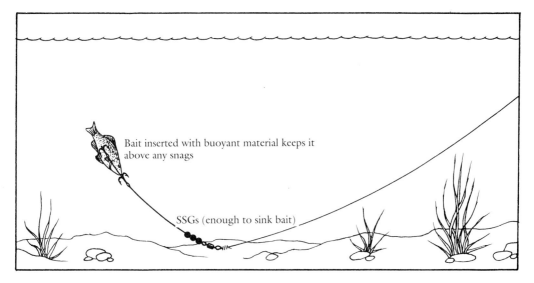

Bait inserted with buoyant material keeps it above any snags

SSGs (enough to sink bait)

Fig. 5.7 Buoyant deadbait.

especially if you want to fish them at any range. When freezing your own baits always ensure they are fresh; lay them out individually on a tray and cover them with a damp cloth; this ensures that they don't dry out. When taking baits out for a day's fishing try to keep them frozen for as long as possible. Wide-necked vacuum flasks are ideal for this job as are the largest boilie bags, if you include a frozen freezer pack when you set off. In my opinion, baits that have been defrosted are not worth re-freezing for future trips; instead, these may be cut up and used as groundbait to avoid wastage.

The types of sea and coarse deadbait available to us today is simply astounding. The list is far too great to mention them all; however, some do seem to be more effective than others. Both herring and mackerel have made an incredible impact over the years, which I suspect is due to the very high oil content contained in these fish. Smelt took the pike world apart several years ago, again I believe because of a very distinct smell, and sandeels

and eel sections have all had more than their fair share of success. I strongly suspect the next "wonder bait" may be garfish, as anyone who has caught this game little sea fish will tell you that it stinks to high heaven and would readily cut up into a section-type bait. The use of exotics has also produced a reasonable amount of success; a number of these tropical reef fish have now become readily available from fishmongers. A good point to bear in mind when buying these fish is that they will always arrive at the fishmonger's frozen, where they will be defrosted for the slab, so it would pay to ask if it were possible to sell them to you still frozen.

Moving on from baits themselves, let's take an in-depth look at the revolution that has changed the use of deadbaits so dramatically. By their nature, deadbaits are ideal for enhancing, both with flavours/attractors and with colours, and methods of applying these are relatively simple. I believe that this type of enhancement will dramatically improve your catch rates but, having said that, it is almost

Steve Harper, the famous Norfolk pike angler, with a couple of deadbaits in the water.

impossible to prove conclusively that any pike caught was the sole result of any additives. As I have already stated, there are two main areas of enhancement both of which rely on the pike's basic feeding instincts. Let's deal with flavours first, as this seems to be the most widely accepted form of enhancement.

Flavours

Having working in a tackle shop for a number of years, my nose has been subjected to some of the worst flavours and oils imaginable but, however unpleasant, I can assure you that they are very effective for pike because scent

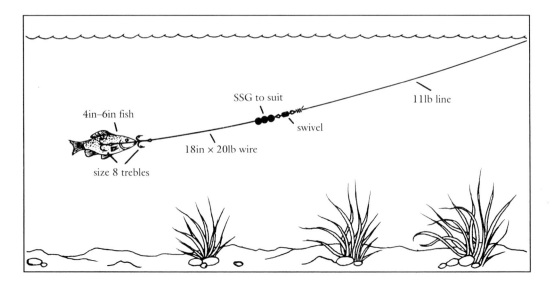

Fig. 5.8 Wobbled deadbait.

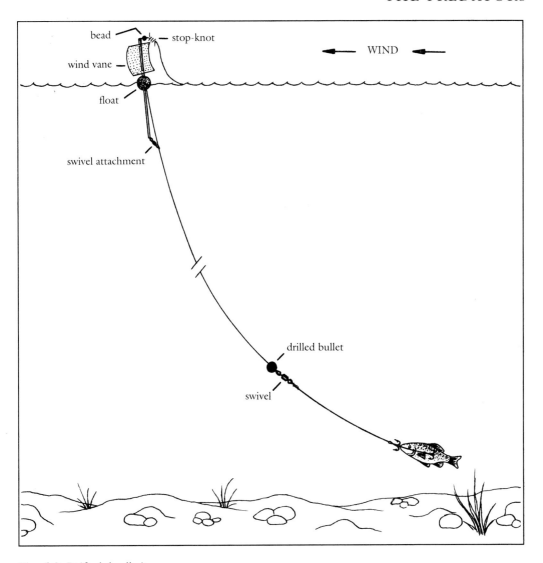

Fig. 5.9 Drifted deadbait.

plays a very big part in their tracking down of a good meal. Smelt is one of a number of fish with a strong smell: get really fresh smelt and you are as good as guaranteed a run.

Most tackle shops now carry a range of liquid pike attractors; these are more often than not oil based and have been produced purely for the pike angler. Companies like Richworth,

E.T. Products and Starmer all market some good attractors, with varieties such as Sturgeon, Shrimp, Scampi, Lobster, Kipper, Enriched Smelt, Prime Scad, Oily Sardine and Grey Mullet all having been put to good use and having caught a large number of fish.

The methods for applying your chosen attractor are relatively simple. The best way

I have found if you require a slow leak off from the bait is to inject either the flavour or oil with a syringe, while a liberal coating on a bait just prior to casting offers a far quicker dispersion into the water but does not last for very long. Swimfeeders filled with foam or cotton wool and soaked in flavours have also proved to be very effective, although these can be awkward to cast if you are fishing at any great distance.

Colours

The second form of enhancement, the visual effect, is becoming increasingly more popular. Over the last few years, the sales of coloured

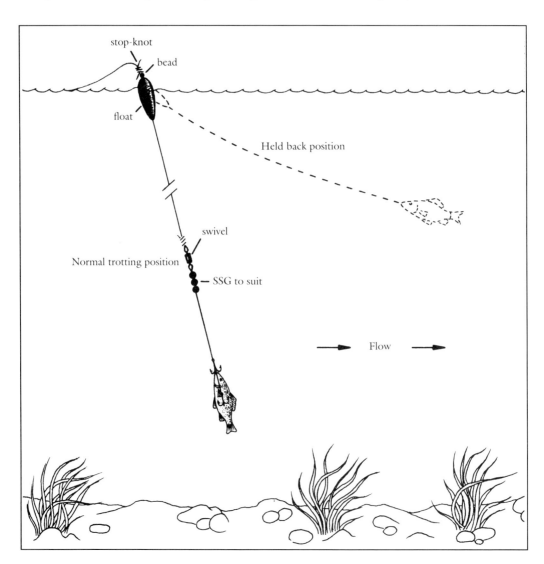

Fig. 5.10 Trotted deadbait.

deadbaits through the tackle shops have soared. Colouring your own is, again, a fairly easy job. Just take a few fresh baits and soak them overnight in a container, making sure that your chosen colour completely covers the fish; then remove them and freeze in plastic bags of three or four fish per bag.

Over the last year or so a relatively new concept of visual enhancement has become more popular: the use of fluorescence. Fluorescence is not a colour, it is a visual effect, and treated baits are thought to be up to three times more visible than untreated baits. It is in this area that I admit I have a vested interest. Several years of research led me to a product that I now import, Glowbait, and this is, as far as I know, the only product that will actually fluoresce a bait. This effect can also be achieved to a lesser degree by attaching an isotope or starlight to the trace somewhere near the bait, but it does not create a fluorescent "smoke" trail which will drift away from the bait, attracting any pike in the area.

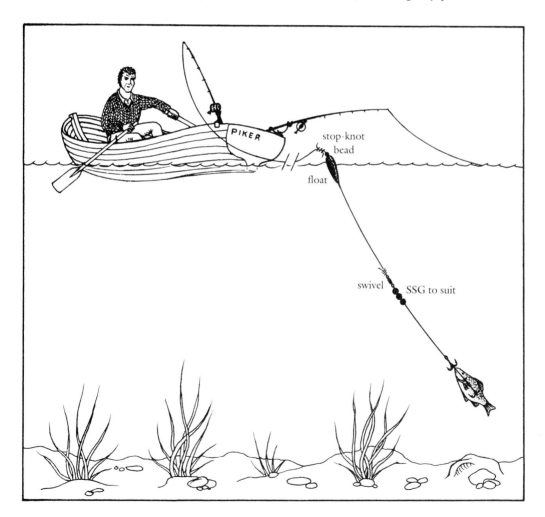

Fig. 5.11 Trolled deadbait.

Feedback I have received from anglers using Glowbait seems to confirm that it is very effective and all have experienced a significant increase in run rates using the fluorescent effect.

Another visual enhancer that I am experimenting with is a flavour additive with glitter in. This, it is claimed, imitates scales falling off an injured fish and the limited tests that I've done so far have proved highly successful.

Overall, it seems that baits fished off the bottom either by paternostering, float fishing or being injected with air on a lead rig have all been far more successful than any baits fished hard on the bottom. Probably the best advice I could give to anyone is to remember that there are no hard and fast rules; it does pay to experiment sometimes and do things differently from others around you; and always remember that no additive, however good, can replace location and good angling skills, it can only help if you have fish in the area to start with.'

FISH BAITS FOR PART-TIME PREDATORS

At certain times of the year many of the less obvious fish species turn at least partly to predatory ways. This habit is far better appreciated and more commonly witnessed on the Continent than here in Britain where the capture of any fish other than perch, pike, zander or eel on fish bait is seen as something of a fluke. The well-known northern grayling fisherman, Mike Mee, told me of large bream that he saw taken on big wet flies in Belgian waters. The locals fishing around him said that there was nothing unusual in these captures in that bream of eight and more pounds frequently took large wet flies meant to imitate small fish. During the 1960s and 1970s, Frans Domhof, the famous Dutch angler, wrote of roach, rudd and bream being taken on spinners in large numbers.

In his book *Successful Roach Fishing*, the late David Carl Forbes wrote: 'I recall being fascinated by the prospects of catching roach by spinning in 1960 and tentatively trying my hand at it, but although I devised dozens of tiny spinners with metal spoons and made bladeless lures of such things as minute glass beads, five or six abortive trips dulled the edge of my enthusiasm. I suspect the problems are not so much from the lures themselves but in finding suitable methods of presentation, for I cannot envisage a roach persisting in chasing small fry. I do believe it will gorge itself on small fry if it can do so without too much effort, but I really cannot see this somewhat portly alderman tearing about with the voracity of a perch, pike or trout. The build of the fish alone makes this unlikely. I have never seen roach actually eating small fish and I have yet to meet anyone who has, but this is no proof that it does not happen.'

So far, this is not very exciting but he does have this to add: 'On one occasion in the early 1960s I wanted to make plaster casts of dace and small chub for identification purposes at lectures to schools and angling clubs. Having cast a 9oz dace, I examined the internal organs and found the stomach crammed with the remains of small fish. Some of these were possibly two inches long and two other anglers witnessed their removal. As I recall, the dace was taken either in January or February. And, following publication of an account of this incident in the magazine *Fishing*, I received a letter from Mr Benjamin Pond, telling me that he regularly took large dace from the River Nadder, Wiltshire, on minnow livebaits!'

The pace hots up, especially when Carl Forbes goes on to say: 'In November 1969 I took a 1lb 14oz grayling from the Hampshire Avon on a minnow livebait put out in relatively deep water for perch. An angler to whom I showed the grayling, with the minnow tail in its throat, refused to believe it was

Chub will eat small fish.

possible and later asserted that it was obviously a case of a grayling accidentally taking a minnow that was picking at a bread or maggot bait. Yet T. K. Wilson, who struck me as knowing a thing or two about graylings, once told me that he considered the best chance of catching a big grayling would come from livebaiting with minnows or small dace.'

Let's examine more evidence. In 1990 I had this to say about a bend on Norfolk's River Wensum: 'There were a great number of fry in the slack at the head of the pool and on milder nights they dimpled the surface constantly. They had obviously attracted pike, for slashing attacks were common in rapid bursts ten minutes or so apart. Well into the winter, something struck me as unusual about these strikes. They seemed too noisy and splashy for pike, I felt, and I began to suspect the possibility of a perch shoal at work. Accordingly, I sat on the bank well away from my rod, my torch beam playing into the clear water. The fry were easily visible, glinting like needles in the top layer of water. I waited a mere five minutes before four shapes glided into the beam, five feet down and rising quickly. They were, of course, big bream and they hit into the fry like bats from Hell's dark depths; chasing, harrying them, and sinking back down with at least one fish each in their mouth. Naturally I tried little live and deadbaits a great deal thereafter and it would be nice, but completely untrue, to say that is how I caught more bream. However, apart from a jackpipe and two eels, nothing else touched them, so it was back to bread and worms and the occasional big fish pulling the quiver-tip round.'

It has long been appreciated that, in the early summer especially, barbel are attracted to feeding on small fish. Peter Stone mentioned this frequently in the 1960s and 1970s and suggested this habit is probably because the barbels' shallow gravel spawning beds are infested by fry, minnows and gudgeon at this

This perch was caught on a gudgeon.

time of the year and so represent an easy source of food. Perhaps this periodic predation of the barbel could also be nature's way of ensuring that they protect at least a percentage of their fertilized eggs from the shoals of many fish that would otherwise decimate them.

Carp, too, become predatorial when for one reason or another their water has become infested with fry and small fish. This seems to be a perfect example of a highly developed fish taking full advantage of any food source opening up.

The message is clear: bream, roach, barbel, carp and even dace, as well as chub and perch will all at times take small fish as a food source, either alive or dead. It seems to me that there are two main questions raised. Firstly, is this happening frequently enough to make purposeful dead or livebait fishing for these species worth while? Secondly, how does a committed and ambitious angler set about presenting these baits in such unconventional circumstances?

A perfect example of when fish baits become very important is during the period of the elver run. During the spring, elvers, or young adult eels about the length of a needle, enter the rivers of the British Isles after their long journey across the Atlantic whence they have been carried by the Gulf Stream. They have undergone several changes during the journey and at once begin their upstream ascent towards the fresh water that will be their home for years. As the water warms in the spring they can be seen at weirs and sluices, glued to the bank and supports, an easy food for many predators. In many cases they are here in their hundreds and thousands and it is at this time that most species of freshwater fish gorge themselves on elver, especially at the height of the run. Even fish not normally considered as predators will join in the feast. In fact, other more usual baits are

A big perch and its prey.

A small fish mauled by a perch.

often ignored when the elvers are really thick in the river. This is a natural phenomenon not unlike the Mayfly rise of trout rivers of early June. During this period, 'Duffers Fortnight', trout are totally preoccupied on the big flies and so it is with chub, dace, roach, barbel and perch when the elvers are on the move.

Elvers for hook-bait can be picked off the weirside or scooped from the shallows in a fine-mesh landing-net or even a child's shrimping net. A good place to catch large quantities of the little eels is in the small pockets of slack water which form behind any underwater obstacles or snags. If you look carefully in to the water you will see what look like long strands of weed. Look closely and these will turn into thousands of tiny elvers working against the current, moving in complete harmony as the water direction changes. The sweep of a large net can provide enough bait for a week. During the summer months a supply of elvers can also be obtained by trapping them in a drop-net baited with fish pieces. Man-made structures such as bridges or weirpools attract them and the trap should be set as near to these as possible. After a couple of hours, raise the net as quickly and smoothly as possible and, if a large supply is required, try to use the net at night when the fish are at their most active.

The elvers can be stored in a bucket with a couple of inches of water at the bottom. If, however, they are to be kept for more than a few hours, some form of flowing water is vital to keep large numbers alive. Elvers can be preserved whole until required for use by deep freezing. Before fishing, take them from the freezer and wash them to make sure they are quite clean and then pack them into a leak-proof box.

This perch took a deadbait.

Fig. 5.12 Bullhead.

Live elvers are very slippery and difficult to hold. Sometimes it is possible to grip them in a dry cloth or even a little dry groundbait on the hands gives a easier hold. They are best lip-hooked on a size 10 or 12 hook. Two or three elvers can be hooked together on a size 6 or 8 to provide a larger bait for a big-mouth chub or good-sized perch.

The best way of fishing the elvers is under a float which will carry them along with the current and work them around midwater. The float should be manoeuvred against bridges, locks, weirs, fallen trees and close to bank sides. It pays to trot the elver down the main flow and then check it so it rises enticingly in the water. Stop it completely and let it drift into an eddy or towards a deep undercut in the bank. The areas that produce the most bites are generally those where the greatest accumulation of elvers has already gathered. It is almost certain that elver-crazed fish will have gathered just away from the main body of the little fish and the hook-bait is likely to be accepted almost at once. Bites are vicious and frequently the elver is whipped from the hook before any strike can be made. Roach in particular are prone to grabbing hold of the elver's tail and tugging the fish free. Chub and perch are more likely to engulf the whole thing head first.

We do not always meet with elver runs, and the question of fish-bait presentation in general conditions and situations remains largely unanswered. What suggestions I can offer are gleaned from other writers, many of whom are friends, and my own personal experience and those of my fishing circle.

There is no doubt that, in June and July, if barbel shoals are on the gravels then one legered minnow on a size 10 hook or even two on a size 6 hook are well worth a try. This is the one time of the year when barbel are actively predatorial and bites are judderingly positive. The same bait and approach work well obviously for chub. Both chub and barbel will also respond to the float-fished dead minnow that is dragged slightly more slowly than the current downstream. Chub will also respond wildly to a rubby-dubby or crushed and minced sprats. This boilie, bloody mixture can be fed into the swim some yards upstream of the fish. The pieces of oily meat trigger an instant response and the float-fished live or dead minnow in the slick should invariably, inevitably, be taken.

A hunting perch shoal is quite easily spotted. Often the dorsal fins break clear which is a total giveaway. Unlike pike, perch will hunt an individual fish for several yards and in general their attacks at a shoal of prey fish tend to be more splashy. A two- or three-inch livebait fished in any attack area is very likely to be taken. In my experience, most livebaits for perch should be lip-hooked and a strike made somewhere between five and ten seconds after the float disappears or the run, if legering, commences. Gudgeon, small roach, small perch or small chub all make perfect big perch baits.

I have already confessed to my problems with catching predatorial bream. I would not consider fishing for bream with small livebaits unless I saw them actively hunting. If this case occurs again I will repeat the experiment, again with minnows, sticklebacks or small fry fished on a size 12 or 14 hook.

And as for roach? It would, of course, be irresponsible to recommend a small live or deadbait for a species so obviously non-predatorial. In 1972 the *Angler's Mail* reported a two-pound plus roach caught on a minnow livebait but this must be seen as the exception, although, undoubtedly, the odd very big fish will turn into a hunter on occasion.

In the 1970s there was much debate on whether carp were predatorial. Several writers noticed that floating crust often attracted small roach and rudd that would flee at the approach of a big carp (Fig. 5.13). The hypothesis was that the carp was actually homing in to attack the small fish. This at the time I felt was doubtful as indeed I still do today. Though I have seen this event happen many times I have yet to witness a small fish

Two live baits accounted for these fish.

Profile of a predator.

Fig. 5.13 A predator attack.

Grayling caught on the fly.

being eaten by an approaching carp. This does not mean that carp do not eat fish. A few years ago a friend in Oxfordshire did exceptionally well legering small chunks of roach and bream in a well-coloured carp lake that was heavily infested with small fish. Using fish chunks on one rod and conventional baits on another he could draw some comparisons, and the fish baits quite steadily scored more heavily. We know that carp like fishmeal and the general taste and flavour of fish so it is quite possible that the texture of the real thing does not deter them. Though boilies have not had their day, it is inevitable that the carp angler tomorrow will be looking for new bait developments and something like fish chunks or pieces could provide an avenue of investigation.

ARTIFICIAL FLIES FOR COARSE FISH

At around 4.30 p.m. on 20 May 1992 I witnessed an extraordinary phenomenon. The day was very hot for the time of the year and was the fifth in a row that the temperatures had been well over 68°F (20°C). I walked around the estate and reached – inevitably – the wildie pond. At first I could see no fish and then I found a good head of them in the southern bay. From a distance, they gave every indication of being engaged in spawning. I got closer and in a few minutes was sure that my first impression was correct. Fish were everywhere, close in to the margins and topping frequently.

It was after five minutes that I began to wonder; the fish were showing none of the orgiastic tendencies associated with spawning. They were rather coming up in a quietly positive fashion, head first, with the back following through and down smoothly. Others were simply kissing the surface of the water, leaving rings and little vortices where they had sipped. I watched several of these actions very closely. I was quite convinced that these carp were deliberately taking things from the surface and after only a few more minutes' exploration I discovered what these were. There was a large hatch of small mosquitoes in the shallow, sun-warmed bay and the carp were sucking in the buzzers as they struggled in the surface film trying to hatch into the mature insect. Despite the extreme murkiness of the water I had no doubt what I was seeing. Some of the fish were only feet from me and I watched them rising and sucking the insects in over and over.

I could hardly expect anyone to believe what I could hardly credit myself. I tried for a long while to take photographs but the hatch was over before I was convinced that I had a conclusive frame of the event. Rising fish became fewer and fewer and a little after 5.15 p.m. I was forced to admit that the spectacle was over, yet I have no doubt that a large artificial buzzer fished just sub-surface would have landed a carp on that particular day.

In 1986, Norfolk's Blickling Lake became very clear indeed, showing the tench to be feeding on the daphnia beds, bloodworm, nymphs and water boatmen. So rich were the supplies of natural food that anglers' baits were all but ignored. Very occasionally a piece of corn or a couple of maggots would be sipped in but this was the exception. Large baits or heavy feeding both proved to be disastrous and tench kept well clear of any noticeably groundbaited areas. As the season developed, it grew more and more frustrating to see large numbers of big tench feeding strongly and yet never look like being caught.

It was at this point that the Bailiff, David Cooper, began to experiment with fly fishing the tench. David is very much a traditional all-round angler, as happy with trout as with tench, and soon he was casting short, neat lines around the shallows over the browsing tench. It would be wrong to suggest that David wiped the board but after initial failures he was soon catching one or two fish each evening while we were struggling for a single fish every two or three sessions with our conventional approach.

Small Pheasant Tail nymphs tied on a size 16 did the damage as I remember. Fished on a 4lb leader they were allowed to sink within a few inches of the bed and then were twitched through the feeding tench. The retrieve had to be slow and takes were gentle but surprisingly positive and he missed few bites. The extreme clarity made the whole operation very exciting and allowed him to place his fly with pinpoint accuracy. By the time algae growth clouded the water and bait began to work again, I was convinced that fly fishing for tench in clear water does have possibilities. It is a matter of great regret that I have not tried this method myself in the intervening years but I will. Of course, the problem is overcoming the initial disbelief and lack of confidence in such a stunningly different approach.

Carp fishermen are no more adventurous: it is close on twenty years ago that Chris Yates wrote an article on fishing artificial moths for the species. It was based on his own detailed observation that during certain conditions, carp would come to the surface to feed on floating insects. Despite this, dry-fly fishing for carp had hardly become a mainstream method and I have never seen anyone practising it.

Surely, though, the method has possibilities. We have all seen carp well on the surface on small waters or in the bays of large ones as the weather warms. Towards evening, a thick scum develops built of dislodged weed, fallen insects, the oil of birds' feathers, the pollen from the trees and the dust from the land. In this, carp love to lie, sucking and blowing at bits of flotsam. Who has not seen a carp suck in a rhododendron bloom, a petal or a struggling cranefly? These must be the times that the artificial fly stands the best chance of success. The game-angling shop sells many moth and cranefly patterns, generally tied on to strong hooks sized 6 to 10. A reservoir or a light salmon rod, a floating no. 8 or 9 line and a 10lb leader should complete the outfit.

Casting might well be a problem on anything apart from a very new pit, but perfect presentation should not be necessary. Most of the flies in the surface scum are fairly flat and battered anyway. Where the trees are simply too thick to allow any fly casting whatsoever, then normal floater fishing tackle could be used with a fly on the point rather than bait. A small bubble float or controller float would give all the necessary weight for casting.

Once the artificial is on the water in the vicinity of carp, I guess the best approach would be to twitch it occasionally so that it sends out warning rings and perhaps even moves a couple of inches. The alternatives are to let it lie completely still or to retrieve it steadily. Everything is worth trying.

The big question is whether this whole method is simply quirky, and likely to appeal only perhaps to eccentrics looking for something new. This is probably so but it could just be the one-off, brainwave approach to a particular, cunning big fish that has seen every bait and every trick but this one over its many years of life.

For many of the remaining species, the efficiency of the artificial fly has long since been proved. There have been, for example, huge amounts of perch caught from trout reservoirs since this branch of the sport really opened up in the 1950s and 1960s. Most of these have fallen to deeper-fished, large lures stripped back quickly for rainbow trout. Before the perch disease, the species was taken from most of the reservoirs but my own experience has been limited to Chew Valley and Ardleigh. At both these waters, large concentrations of perch provided often unwelcome sport for the trout angler and to return them was illegal – a tragic waste of lovely fish often averaging two pounds or more. Those I caught or saw caught fell to typical rainbow lures – bright flashy flies, tied on hooks sized 6 to 12. Whiskies, Jersey Herds, Appetizers,

Baby Dolls, Dog Knobblers and many, many more creations all scored spectacularly and at times a shoal would give itself up. At Chew especially, it would not be unusual to see a dozen fish littering the ground around a single angler.

The continuing success of flies at these waters cannot be anything like a total fluke. Large numbers of fish and very clear water were probably instrumental but neither of these factors is unusual. My own belief is that flies are often very much more attractive to perch than spoons or plugs. Metal and plastic do not have the fluid, wavering, shimmering realism of fur and feather. A fly releases bubbles as it works, looking every bit like some alive struggling creature. A fly, furthermore, is soft and flesh-like when it is mouthed and therefore much less likely to be immediately rejected. Never would I rate flies higher than livebaits or even deadbaits for perch but I do feel they could be on a par with worms for big fish and in many circumstances they must have the beating of artificial lures.

Excellent rudd flies are the Black Gnat, the Wickham's Fancy and the Coachman, all ties on hook sizes 12 to 16. None of these will catch a fish more than once. I do not believe that these dry flies, or any of the many others that work well, will catch a rudd more than once and I principally use them as a change bait when mixers, crust pieces and cat biscuits have begun to wane.

Chub are a little more obliging than rudd on many occasions, especially on clear, shallow quick rivers that are not overfished, and will fall to a dry fly once or twice before avoiding them thereafter. Zulus are good, big Coachmen too, and there are times when they will go crazy for artificial Craneflies or Mayflies.

Not every coarse fisherman could regard the grayling as his natural territory which is a great shame for no fish is more beautiful, fights more heartily or is more difficult at times to tempt. Obviously, grayling could be caught on the usual worms and maggots but there are times when flies work at least as well. Many years ago I had some spectacular fishing on the River Tweed and wrote about it at the time:

'The river was cold as I searched it, turning over its stone-lined bottom, hunting out the food store of the gravels. Waterfleas for the most part, small shrimps, several snail families, nymphs in plenty and many caddis. Looking at the squirming samples in hand, I felt a small dark Pheasant Tail was as fair an imitation of any of these blob lives as anything else. My first cast of the new day snaked out and, as before, bellied with the flow. I watched the leader along every knot, over every boulder with a burning intensity for action – that came so fast, so dramatically that the take of the fish could be heard, quite loud as it slashed the line tight through the water.

The fish was plunging, revolving on its back, gleaming its slim yellow body, hanging in the current, arrowing away in short thrusts and rattling the rod tip. Yard by yard the rod worked it into the shallows, where it swam higher in the water, where the proud dorsal of a big grayling is extended. I could watch her fight in the now sunlit, clear water.

My style of fishing produced takes that made my blood freeze. I was, almost, trotting the flow like a float man on the Trent after roach or gudgeon. I worked the fly hard, lifting it, while holding it back enough to bring a grayling in on it with a barnstorming lunge, zipping the line tight, violent as a sea trout. After I had been given two or three chances, or fish, the shoal would move and so would I, downstream until I found them or, failing that, I would return to the top of the run once more. It was important to let the fish settle between times whilst I read or watched the valley life roll by.'

It would be foolish to end this section on fly fishing for coarse fish without mentioning the use of the natural flies. Obviously, chub, rudd, carp and roach are quite happy to take live flies off the surface in certain conditions. So, too, are dace. Richard Walker, in fact, made quite a science of catching dace on the fly, devising a special float for the job. He immersed a swan quill in hot water to soften it and then put a piece of lead into the quill. When the quill had cooled and dried, it held the lead firmly in position at the point of balance. This streamlined, internally weighted float cast very efficiently and landed on the water with little commotion. It also offered less resistance in the strike than a bubble float.

'Just before the float lights,' says R. W. 'the line should be checked to cause the fly to fall below and beyond the float. Then a further check after the float hits the water will allow the fly to go well ahead of it, before they both start on their way towards the fish. But we realize that a study of the current must be made to ensure that the right spot is chosen to start the swim-down with it virtually trotting as in float fishing.

As that tackle glides downstream, keep just in touch with the float without checking it. This, though not difficult, is a somewhat delicate operation which demands one's whole attention. I have not found it necessary to strike very fast to hook even small dace when fishing in this way. They hold the natural fly much longer than they would hold an artificial, which, however, can be used as desired though it is not nearly as effective. Dead flies can also be used, but they lack the attractive twizzle of the live ones.'

Indeed, it is this 'attractive twizzle' that makes the use of live flies so attractive. There is no doubt that as they struggle they send out rings that all species find almost irresistible. Past writers have recommended the use of a wide range of flies: bumble-bees, ladybirds, butterflies, grasshoppers and craneflies have all been used over the years. My own feeling is that these exotics are not absolutely necessary and in some cases are approaching rarity. In my own view, it is quite sufficient to buy half a pint of maggots, let them turn to casters and then hatch out into bluebottles or close relatives. These flies are invariable big, juicy and active, and nature is not raided in the least. The flies are quite large enough to take a size 12 or even size 10 hook nipped in through the back. Provided the job is done carefully, a large fly will remain active for quite a number of minutes providing the cast is done gently and does not destroy it upon impact with the surface.

A long rod is always an advantage when fishing the natural fly as it gives the greatest possible control whether trotted or fished out on the wind in a still water. A controller float of some sort is generally essential – either of the modern carp-fishing variety or the simple old bubble float.

Chub tend to take the surface-fished bluebottle with a great splash, probably frightened of losing it at the last moment. Rudd, too, are equally positive, while most dace will splash at a large bluebottle once or twice, hoping to down it and secure a better hold in their much smaller mouths. For carp, I would consider using craneflies – good old daddy-long-legs – in preference to bluebottles. Many times I have seen carp browsing in surface scum towards the end of the day sucking in items of food, among which are drowning craneflies. Once more, this is the occasional method that could just conceivably land that large wary fish.

I have never had a roach take a natural fly of mine from the surface, but I have had limited success by legering a fly. In 1991, the upper River Bure was very clear and the roach shoals were correspondingly cautious. All normal baits were treated with extreme caution until one particular day I resorted to trotting a dead bluebottle in midwater. Success was not dramatic or absolute but two good fish were taken on a day when bread and maggots and casters had all been refused.

There should not be anything surprising about these successes on natural fly. We know, as we have known for centuries, that all coarse fish eat natural flies as a large part of their diet; it is simply that bait has become so readily available from modern tackle shops that many of us are unwilling to try anything novel. Just perhaps, reading this book will change that for some, more pioneering anglers. I hope so. There is a satisfaction in catching a fish in a different way and proving and disproving a theory. After all, fishing is about fun and learning and we have still a great deal to discover in both fields.

In Germany barbel like this are taken on nymphs.

Index